A Memoir

Edward A. Nichols, M.D.

FADE TO WHITE

iUniverse books may be ordered through booksellers or by contacting:

iUniverse
1663 Liberty Drive
Bloomington, IN 47403
www.iuniverse.com
1-800-Authors (1-800-288-4677)

ISBN: 978-1-4917-4150-4 (sc)
ISBN: 978-1-4917-4283-9 (hc)
ISBN: 978-1-4917-4138-2 (e)

Library of Congress Control Number: 2014913212

Printed in the United States of America.

iUniverse rev. date: 12/12/2014

This book is written in praise of my mother, Maude Christina Atkinson Nichols, the epitome of courage, who defended her two sons and raised them into manhood in the forties and fifties. It is the story of her struggle with racism and her stoic ride in adversity. She had to pass for white in order to get a position as secretary to an army colonel in the Army Supply Corps during the war. I remember meeting her in a fancy white restaurant downtown and watching lots of heads turn when she called out, "Son, here I am!"

CONTENTS

PREFACE

My interest in writing a memoir first came from discussing my daughters' questions about race. As we sat in the garden on what was meant to be a lazy Sunday, Christy and Meredith, my teenage daughters, began to interrogate me. The subject of their curiosity was our family history. My daughters are biracial children, and they wanted a more fully fleshed, less fragmented understanding of their ancestry. This natural adolescent curiosity about genealogy was heightened by issues of personal identity and ancestry.

Christy and Meredith decided the best starting point would be a more detailed understanding of my childhood in the small, isolated colored world of the Bronx circa 1950. They asked many, many questions that day. Some—indeed, quite a few—I could not answer. Early afternoon turned to dusk, and it became clear that the more I reminisced, the more confused they became. Something—someone—was missing in the telling.

I understood their confusion. Over the last fifty years, much of my interior life has been consumed with attempts to fill in the blanks and contradictions in my family history. Of course, gaps in multigenerational family history are not an uncommon legacy for many African American families. Still, the missing person in my case was not at some generational remove but was much more immediately related. Uncovering the mysteries of my father—Leon Terrenze Nichols, my children's grandfather—has remained the consuming enigma in my life.

My father had left my mother when I was a boy, and I was always hoping one day to track him down and get some answers to my many questions.

My recollections of my father are framed in a series of fleeting images fixed during one week in the spring of 1943, when he returned home on furlough. I have a seminal, somewhat shifting memory of meeting my father in the vast caverns of Penn Station. In another recollection I find myself running beside him as he walked to the local liquor store on Boston Road. My most detailed and powerful recollection is the day he came to my school. He stood six feet two inches tall, resplendent in his officer's uniform as Mrs. Marge Mann, my third-grade teacher, introduced him to the admiring audience of PS 78. A medal pinned to his breast pocket testified to bravery in the rescue that followed his ship being torpedoed in the South Pacific. I don't recall any other time when a neighborhood resident with an officer's rank has ever been so proudly shown off. It was even more impressive because my father was black. In 1943, most of the students and all of the teachers at the Anne Hutchinson School, PS 78—in fact, pretty much all of Williamsburg—were white.

Then, just as his leave was winding down, I overheard a terrible argument between him and my mother. My father stormed out of the house. My mother, my brother, and I would never see or hear from him again. It seemed as if he had walked out the door, floated into the air above our home on 3581 Fish Avenue, and vanished forever. For years, no one knew if he was dead or alive. Later it seemed that my mother did indeed know where he was, but that is another story.

As I grew from boyhood into manhood and tried to find out about my father, I continually met with frustrating non-news from family members. My mother never allowed my older brother—my only sibling—or me to talk about our father; she, of course, never mentioned him, except to say, "There is nothing to say." No one else in the family ever talked about him either, and so presumably, no one knew the real—and, I might add, shocking—truth about the man who had sired me. Equally frustrating had been a series of dead-end attempts to locate him on my own. Just finding out if he was even alive had been impossible. And as the years went by—through my marriages, the births and raising of my three daughters, and the evolution of my career as a doctor—all the while I continued to feel that an important part of my life was still missing.

By a stroke of luck and destiny, we finally got some answers, and then we had to look for more answers. The questions I asked, and that my daughters came to ask, and the answers I uncovered are the main purposes of this memoir.

But my story is about my search for my father and how it affected my life. I will also write about my life, education, profession, and thoughts about the world I live in. I will try not to meander too much, but all of it is connected by the same theme: my father and me.

Chapter One

EARLY LIFE IN THE BRONX

Williamsbridge

In the 1940s many of the streets in Williamsbridge were paved with a mixture of coarse gravel and tar, and there were many empty lots from Gun Hill to 233rd. There were hundreds of "victory gardens" of different shapes and sizes where old Italian and black men built crude shacks and grew all kinds of vegetables of the new and old countries so that they could eat fresh veggies, which were scarce during the war. There were also the many empty lots where we played baseball and touch football. We had names for them, but I can only remember "Moose Field."

We lived on an oasis between the thousands of Jews living in the Hillside Homes to the east of Fish Avenue and the thousands of Italian and Irish families that lived to the west. (Indians to the left and Indians to the right. Just like Custer at the Little Big Horn.) We were surrounded by a sea of white people. The stationery stores were owned and operated by the Jews, and there were kosher and Italian butcher shops. There were only white teachers at my school; the cops were all white and mostly Irish; the garbage collectors were all white, usually Italian and Polish. Even the conductors on the trains and the drivers on the buses were all white—again, usually Italian or Irish. I didn't know what Negroes and colored people did for a living except singing and dancing and being maids and butlers in the movies. Racial incidents were few but mean-spirited. One white kid came up to me while I was walking on Fish

Avenue through the Hillside Homes apartments and said, "I could put mud on my face and look just like you." A constant inquiry was "Why don't you go back to where you came from?"

I did have some white friends until I was fifteen, and then that was the cutoff. I remember going to a party in Hillside Homes with Letty Joseph, Arnold Spector, and Jeanne Massey and playing spin the bottle. When I would win, the girl would become petrified. When we went into the other room to kiss, she would say, "*Pretend.*" I didn't think it was racist then, but of course it was. With the other white kids, we did play in the playgrounds, and I didn't have any fights. We played a game called "Johnny on the Pony" and handball. Of course we played marbles and "Chestnut Kill" (or whatever the name of the game was). We would soak chestnuts in some liquid vinegar? to harden them and then drill a hole into each and put a string though it. Each player would try to break the other guys' chestnuts by slamming his chestnut into theirs.

We practically lived on the stoops. We read, drank sodas, talked, chatted, argued, and played stoopball and checkers in the hazy, humid, hot days of summer. This was our refuge. When we had played stickball, baseball, and basketball during the day, we would play ring-a-levio or hide-and-go-seek at night. The girls played hopscotch and jumped rope, some better than others, especially double Dutch.

There were islands of black people interspersed with Italians, Jews, and Irish lower-middle-class people. Bronx people were the salt of the earth the loyal union Democrats in sanitation, construction, civil servants, state and local government workers. The Italians were into sanitation, masonry, bricklaying, and plumbing. The Irish were truck drivers and police. The salt of the earth. The islands of black people knew each other, and there were other islands where we had no contact. We were later to learn they experienced similar episodes and had parallel lives. My social contacts were from the block I lived on, the neighboring blocks, and also around the St. Luke's Episcopal Church community. Many, if not most, of the parishioners were West Indians, and the rest were recent arrivals and early groups from South and North Carolina.

I don't remember many details of the summers in the Bronx except that they seemed like an endless game. As I mentioned earlier, We played basketball, stickball, and softball during the day and hide-and-go-seek at night. The schoolyard was locked, but we found a hole in the fence that we crept through. We would play there until the cops came in their patrol cars (probably called by the people of Hillside Homes), and we would scatter. If they caught us, they would take our stickball bats and break them in the sewers. (But there were always other broomsticks.)

I recall many occasions of sneaking through the fence into the schoolyard and also often running into the stoop in front of the house. I was so eager and dumb. My older brother Skippy reminded me that we played basketball in the back schoolyard as well as different types of handball, bounce ball, hardball and stoopball.

When were weren't playing ballgames, we rode bicycles all over the neighborhood, and on one historic occasion we rode to Stamford, Connecticut. And we were exhausted by the attempt. Once we even rode to Edgecombe Avenue on Sugar Hill. When it was too hot to play stickball or softball, we went to Orchard Beach in the Bronx or Jacob Riis in Queens. We rode the train for two hours, hanging on the straps, riding between cars, walking up and down the train cars, and going to the front of the train to lookout the window. Many boys and girls growing up in the outer boroughs of New York have had this delightful and exciting, albeit dangerous, adventure.

In the fall, we played marbles and flew kites and played yo-yo. Skippy and the older guys liked Halloween because he could fill stockings with chalk and beat girls and cars with them. He doesn't remember that I almost burned down our house with a lit pumpkin that I put on the window ledge and that almost set fire to the curtain. Our other neighbor, Sylvia Carr said we would play hide-and-seek and jump rope and play potsy (hopscotch). We spent many nights on the stoops in front of our houses on Fish Avenue, harmonizing songs like "Swing Low, Sweet Chariot" and "You Gotta Have a Dream" and wondering about life. We talked about playing different sports and what we were going to do tomorrow. We rarely talked about the future—at that time, we lived in the present.

People I grew up with often asked me about my feelings about not having a dad around. I didn't feel angry that my father was not with me. Between the ages of six and eight, while I was growing up in the Bronx, I was aware and accepted without anger that he was a "soldier" and would come back to see us when he could. I was told this by a loving and nurturing mother. I accepted this and was in fact so proud when I did see him home on furlough with his officer's uniform and medals.

I repeated the truths—but also the lies and half-truths—that I was told. He was serving in the South Pacific. "I heard that he was on a PT boat." "His boat was torpedoed, and he was saved, although wounded." "He got a medal after the boat was sunk." "He was an officer in the navy."

It was only later, when I was a preteen and teenager, when the war was over and it was apparent that he wasn't coming back with the other soldiers, that my mother explained that they had separated. I see from some of the papers that we later found that my mother was I indeed in contact with a lawyer, but I did not turn up any divorce papers. Even then, I had no anger toward him or my mother. I knew and had heard of several families that had divorced parents. I was nonetheless curious about why and how they separated. I never did get any answers to those questions. (And I had my own egocentric issues as a teenager.) I had to endure that calamity when it was so common among families during the Second World War. So we were not too terribly odd. Later I heard in many war movies about Dear John letters.

As a preteen and teenager, In my adolescent years I lived with the ineffable feeling that something important was missing in my life. I wondered about my father often. When disaster stuck, real or imagined, I longed for the comfort of a father's hug or encouraging smile.

Many children had an imaginary friend; I had an imaginary father. I characterized him most often as a composite of heroes I'd read about. I envisioned him as a Hollywood father figure à la Spencer Tracy or Gregory Peck. Yes, these heroes were white, but during my youth there were few high-profile black heroes other than Joe Louis and Jackie Robinson—whom white people said I looked like. I didn't think so. Nor did I want to be a prizefighter or a baseball player.

My mother—Mother Maude, as I called her—was beautiful, graceful, and intelligent. During the war years she worked as a secretary for the Army Ordnance Department at Tremont Avenue.

Maude Atkinson Nichols circa 1945

Later she would become a supervisor for the IRS. Each workday evening at a quarter after six, I would meet her bus at Wilson Avenue and Boston Post Road, and we would walk home together. It could not have been easy raising two boys alone. My brother and I could be more than a notion. She had to be a strict disciplinarian in fulfilling the roles of mother and father. Mother Maude was ever vigilant in observing and teaching us manners. Her lessons and dictums were rigidly enforced with icy glares of authority.

There were moments when she felt overwhelmed. I remember hearing her talk to her girlfriend, whom we called "Aunt Helen": "I am so exhausted and might have to put one of them in a home this summer," she said. At least that was what I told my brother Skippy. "She's going to put you in a home," and he countered, "She's talking about you."

5

Aunt Helen calmed her down. That's when we started going to summer camps every summer.

Mother Maude's boyfriends, Sy MacArthur and Capt. Ted Thompson were our role models. Sy was chief steward on the SS *United States*. Thompson was a captain in the military police stationed in the US Army prison at Nuremberg and later at the 135th Street Military Police in Harlem. Later he was police commissioner in the US Virgin Islands. So we had role models for discipline. Sy was also very kind to us boys. He had been raised in an orphanage and was sensitive to our needs. He bought us Harris Tweed suits and jackets from Mark Schafer on Madison Avenue. Years later, as an adult, I visited Ted Thompson in the Virgin Islands. I called him at the number listed in the phone book when I was visiting friends in St. Thomas, and he came over in a sea plane to visit with me and my family. We chatted for hours about my mother Maude and Skippy and our lives since he knew us. He died three months later.

Maude with Captain Ted Thompson

***

Like many children I grew up vacillating between moments of self-admiration and self-doubt. Encyclopedias and newspapers were my reading of choice. I was often bored with school, distracted in class, and frequently called a rascal by adults whose patience I had exhausted.

Skippy and I had our share of fights and sibling rivalry. When he wanted to annoy me, he addressed me as White Fang because of my occluded teeth. He was three years older, far bigger and stronger, and when he could catch me, he invariably beat the hell out of me. I learned to run very fast. I owe my high school track letter to this early preparation.

A word or two about my elementary school. PS 78 was situated directly across from my house but had the address of 1400 Needham Avenue around the corner. I started school in September 1942 and graduated after seven years in 1949. It was a good school; performance was everything, and there were no discipline problems or guns or drugs in those days. In school I was the only "colored" person in my class. There were other "coloreds" in the school, but they were apparently scattered by design. In any event, there were no overt racial incidents that made any lasting impression. Which means there were none because I would have remembered any incident. We played nicely together in the schoolyard every day and played games in the gym when not in the classrooms. I do remember problems that I had with teachers. There were personal issues between the teacher Mrs. Eskridge and me in September 1943. For example I flunked a big spelling bee in 2A2 because—fresh boy that I was—I pronounced the word *Penelope* "Pen-a–lope." I was called wrong and kicked out of the spelling bee. I was being fresh, and I deserved it. But I do remember the incident and how unhappy I was at the time. I thought it was personal. She dismissed me for being fresh not for spelling incorrectly.

I had cavities when I was in 2A and was given a D in Health Education because I didn't have a dental certificate. I had several cavities in my youth and had to go to Dr. Thaler, the dentist down the street on Fish Avenue. I was born in a time before fluoride toothpaste and fluoridation of the water and had the then normal number of cavities and fillings. I mention Dr. Thaler because of what he told me years later. He said that that he "didn't have a special time or entrance for colored people like some of the other dentists." These islands of memory remain in the sea of the unconscious.

In 3B, because of my behavior at school, my favorite teacher wrote in my report card "works well with other pupils" but also noted the grade "needs work."

At other times I would use the vernacular slang terms that were used "by us colored," like saying something was "bad" when we meant that it was good or calling something a "black lie" when others would say "white lie."

But the big moment was one with Mrs. Jereme. We would never get along, She was such a strong-willed person, and then there were my feelings. I was so bored in her homeroom and music class that I would frequently read the *Daily News*. In any event we had a run-in over something banal, and she called me to her desk at the front of the class. She started to lay me out verbally. I could not bear the strain. As I walked away, I threw her books, which were sitting on the desk, onto the floor. She demanded that I pick them up, and I refused. That landed me in the principal's office.

I was always obnoxious. Shirley Hilliman, one of the neighborhood girls who went to PS 78, said,

> Remember the times you would get into trouble and your teacher would put you in my classroom to 'cool off'? At those times we were the only two black kids in the room, maybe three. Basil Thomas may have been there also. I was always glad to see someone I knew that looked like me and of course felt that your teacher was wrong and you were right. I was in fifth or sixth grade and you were in seventh or eighth. You would proceed to sit in the back of the room and fall asleep (or pretend to).

I wonder now what was going on in my life that made me so angry? Was I missing my father's attention? Shirley wrote in a letter to me that I was, in her opinion, "an angry conceited boy, extremely bright, good looking and you hated girls unless they were light-skinned [she was dark skinned; how sad she thought that of me] there were times however when you were a good friend in a big brother sort of way."

I was often easy to resent. There were moments of self-admiration and other moments of self-doubt. It would be presumptuous of me to think that everyone liked me. I was often arrogant and proud. Others would have called me a brat. It depends on your viewpoint. I thought I was smarter than most, and that did not go over too well. I read encyclopedias and newspapers. I was bored with the school lessons and was often told by my teachers to pay attention. I was called many names as a young boy and teenager; "rascal" rings a bell.

As an adult, I visited my old school PS 78 on Needham Avenue and was amazed at how small the rooms and hallways were. The auditorium was not so big either. I remember lots of shows that we had there including the one in which I was dressed as an Indian brave and we sang a song around a teepee. We wore dungarees and sneakers. I had a feather in my headband.

***

My classmates Alan Applebaum, Norman Decker, and Susan Furman from PS 78 were all smart kids who scored high in IQ tests (above 145). I spent afternoons with fat Alan Applebaum and skinny, wistful Norman Decker at their homes in Hillside Homes. We would all become doctors. There was another student, Eddie Munoz, who was Cuban. He was the only Hispanic I ever knew at that time.

My brother, my friends, and I had our seasonal rituals. At the first sign of a significant snowfall, we would all assemble with Red Flyer or makeshift sleds to assault the steep, three-block-long Hicks Street hill. And "The Great Snowball Fight of '48" continues to live in Williamsburg lore as a testimony to that year's monstrous blizzard.

In the summer, we used pea shooters to blow "pities"—the seeds from the wild cherry trees in our backyards—and terrorize the passing girls. And I still recall the constant reminder not to "track that mess" into the house when the heat caused the gravel and tar of Bronx streets to bubble and stick to sneakers and sandals.

One of our neighbors, Mr. Jackson, introduced me to gardening. His victory garden was one of the hundreds of small plots in our heavily Italian neighborhood. Each boasted a makeshift shack for storing tools, as well as a chair or two for meditation, all just a stone's throw from home. Under Mr. Jackson's tutelage, I learned to garden. Soon our backyard began to sprout a regular crop of lettuce, tomatoes, and string beans. Mother Maude could count on much of what was harvested from my efforts.

Because my grandmother never allowed her girls in the kitchen—to this day I don't know why—mother was not much of a cook. She taught herself to cook a few things well, and Sundays were devoted to preparing her basic menus: fried chicken, a large casserole of macaroni, a large pot of rice, a large pan of fried pork chops, string beans, mashed potatoes, and sometimes candied yams. That would carry us through week. All this would be stored in the "icebox" (i.e., the refrigerator). Skippy and I would usually assemble our meals in the evening and warm them up on a double boiler. We tried not to leave any dirty dishes because there was an army of voracious roaches that would take over when the lights were off. True to her Southern roots, Maude also cooked cornbread and biscuits. Yes, we had collard greens too. I was astonished to read in *Albion Seed* by David Hackett Fischer of Cornell University that the early settlers of the Chesapeake Bay area ate the same soul food that black people eat today. The result of all that was that Skippy and I have never cared for leftovers—even in the age of microwaves. We have never been epicures, but we have been fussy about our food. Years later I brought this up with many parents in the practice who had similar stories about their mothers during WWII.

When I was about ten, I was evidently obnoxious to some or even most because of my constant questions and comments about things I wanted to talk about. At a reunion some years ago that I had at my home, I had an interesting exchange with my of my brothers' constant companions. Corky Anderson said, "Yeah, I remember how you used to ask so many questions, your mother had to buy you an encyclopedia to shut you up." Well, that was an interesting way to put it. I still ran my mouth after getting the encyclopedias, but I had more facts to back me up. In 6A I would do the *New York Daily News* crossword puzzle often in Mrs. Jereme's class and at home and on the front stoop. I would ask anyone and everyone to help with the answers I did not know. For instance, "What is a mine entrance?" I'd ask so many people for answers, but they would say, "I don't do crosswords" or "I don't have time for that." Remember, there were no computer programs, Google, or Internet to give the answers or help find a word or phrase. No one on the block could help me, which was why I got the first small encyclopedia and later the *Encyclopedia Britannica* and the *Merriam-Webster Dictionary*.

The Neighbors on Fish Avenue

The Blanks family lived in the house on the corner of Fish and Hicks Street. Mr. Blanks was a large, brusque man with a bad temper. He was a mailman who lived with his wife and three children. Elihu was a diver at Evander Childs High School and later a dentist, Winifred??, a large, red-headed, freckle-faced girl, was so loud and brash. Their older sister was named Cecelia. Mr. Blank would always yell at us to get off his stoop when we were talking or harmonizing there. We liked to sing "Old Man River" and "Swing Low, Sweet Charriot" and "Go Down, Moses" along with the Ink Spot songs.

The Andersons lived upstairs with their son Karl "Corky" Anderson, who was then and even now so outspoken, critical, and often cynical and mean-spirited. Sylvia Carr kept in contact with him and brought us news about him until his death some months ago. He had become a financial planner but had interesting intelligence jobs before that. Mr. Jackson was an elegant, scholarly man—a tailor who had a beautiful flower garden in the shade under a large oak tree. Mr. Sims lived in the basement; he kept a fancy car in the garage. Mr. Hilliman, a tall, proud, handsome man from British Guiana, was a lawyer; and short, lively Mrs. Hilliman was a schoolteacher. Their daughter was destined to become a teacher and then a principal. The Carrs lived next door to me; the father was a butcher. Further on, lived the Murrels and then the Townsends,(The father was black, and the mother was French). The Townsends kept to themselves behind lace curtains.

The Thomases, who lived directly across the alleyway, were devout Catholics. They had many children including Rhea, Muriel, Betty, Maceo, Roddy, Ruthy, Elena, Basel, and Paul. Mr. Thomas was a prominent Catholic layman and former treasurer of the Harlem Branches of the YMCA and the Urban League. He was a Cornell graduate and a Dobbins-Trinity coal and oil company executive. (According to the *People's Voice*, his income was $5,000 in 1942.) Mrs. Thomas was named Catholic Mother of the Year in 1952. In fact that is what made them so memorable to me. They exposed me to their religion and invited me to talk to a Jesuit priest at one of their parties in the backyard. We had a long memorable conversation about the Ten Commandments.

Mr. Carr was a butcher and owned a butcher shop on Lenox Avenue (Seventh Avenue in Harlem). He lived with his wife, Harriet, and their cute, diminutive, winsome, smart, witty daughter, Sylvia. She married a Danish guy named Jenson and lived in Denmark for a while. Mr. Carr had an MBA from NYU and was interested in black enterprise. He was so successful in Harlem that the gangsters stepped in with their unions and broke up his empire. He then joined the butcher's union and worked on Bathgate Avenue in the Bronx and later on 122nd Street at St. Nicholas Avenue until he retired. They moved to Fish Avenue in 1948. Sylvia was delightful to talk to. And we have kept in touch. She reminded me of her blonde girlfriend Madeline Cooke whom I unsuccessfully chased around constantly. She told me that one time I recited the Song of Solomon to them in her basement. We talked at length about retirement and where we would live; both of us are convinced that there's no place like home and we could always vacation somewhere in the winter.

The Murrels were schoolteachers. Mrs. Murrell was a proud member of the Delaney family, who were famous among "bourgie" colored people. One of their relatives was the late Prof. E. Franklin Frazier, who wrote the book *Black Bourgeoisie*, a scathing portrait of the black middle class.

Mr. Murrell was a teacher as well. Sylvia Carr told me that Edward Murrell is living in Mendocino, California, teaching mathematics. He graduated as an aeronautical engineer from Rensselaer Polytechnic Institute. Nanny teaches in Oakland and has a daughter, Nondi, who is a director at MGM. Mrs. Murrell died in 1993. Bill, who is now over fifty years old, is a school principal in a suburb of Detroit, Michigan.

The Jackson family lived upstairs with their children Joan, Harold, and Marlene. They were very conservative and did not want their children playing on the streets with us. Harold became a preacher. Marlene was a small, thin girl who developed into a beautiful young lady.

The Townsends were a mixed couple: a French woman and a very dark black man. They had a daughter named Gwendolyn who was older than us. Mrs. Townsend kept a beautiful garden in the back yard and would scoop horse manure dropped from the carts of Italian fruit peddlers and scissor sharpeners. Upstairs from them was another mixed couple whose son, Arthur Jackson, did play with us. The last house was occupied by Wendell Pannell whose uncle was the famous black actor Canada Lee (he appeared in the film *Lifeboat*).

Good fences made good neighbors. We, the children, felt that we were an entity, but as far as I and Skippy can remember, the parents never got together or planned anything together. (Shirley Hilliman remembers this differently, however in her later letters to me.) They were all such different people with different backgrounds, different colors, different everything—there was no harmony, I remember only that they would have stoop conversations when the weather permitted. But I would never see any of them in my house or in the backyard to eat.

Around the corner on Needham Avenue, Eloise and Viola Coleman lived with their mother and their brother, Arthur. Arthur never worked a day in his life, and when his mother died, he lived with his sisters. The girls were our babysitters also. We still get together with Eloise at reunions and Skippy's summer barbecues.

On the other side of Fish Avenue on Hicks Street in the Hillside Homes were the tall Nagy brothers who were Jewish. We knew Marshall Nagy, who had several large fish tanks filled with live bearers like mollies and platies and fancy guppies that darted among the forest of *Vallisneria* plants. They were responsible for my lifelong love of tropical fish.

Mark and Bob Rona, who were also Jewish, were our friends too; their mother was so horrified that her sons played with us that she moved them to California in 1950. Skippy told me that Bob Rona died in an automobile accident, and Mark called and came back to see Skippy often. He was for a time a mayor in some small city in California and still calls Skippy once a year.

There are so many other things that I have to remember about the summers in the Bronx, and I'm sure I will with time. There were the smells and colors of the different seasons. I remember the Mars Bars, Good and Plenty, licorice sticks, and other sticks that looked like spirals. I remember breaking each other's walnuts.

During our morning strolls along the streets of Hillside Homes, which was built in the thirties by the Metropolitan Insurance Company, we looked for toys thrown away by angry parents. We searched the garbage cans diffidently; every Friday we would find a treasure trove of junk and bring it to the shack that we had built in the vacant lot behind the property line of our houses. We got the lumber for the shack from the many abandoned houses that were started and then left vacant in the neighborhood. Evidently financing the construction had run into problems after the war. When we were finished scavenging and playing with the toys, we made a bonfire of the old furniture.

We also went to the forest and hills around Edenwald and the swamps and tidewater to catch minnows and tadpoles. We would play hide and seek on Pearsall Avenue where there were large concrete pipe sections. Mr. Perry had a home and small farm there with chickens goats, pigs and what ever else was on his farm.

Shirley remembers frequent cookouts in the backyards and Christmas and New Year's parties at either the Carrs', the Murrells', or her house, to which everyone was invited. Our block was like a family. The adults would discipline us as if they were our parents. We might have resented it, but at the time it gave us a great sense of security in light of the two strongly ethnic neighborhoods we were sandwiched between. We knew we could run to any house in time of trouble.

Shirley wrote to me:

> Remember your dog "Spot." He was my dog and Mr. Jackson would not let us keep him. You happened to be outside when we were taking him to the ASPCA and you asked my Mother if you could have him. I think you hid him in your house for a few days before asking your Mother. Your mother said you and Spot was your best friends for many years. Typical boy and his dog story. After rescuing my dog from the ASPCA you became my hero (smile). All in all, we were all spoiled upper middle class kids. Spoiled in a good sense for we felt we could achieve anything we wanted to. The adults on our block were good role models even with our faults and they gave us a sense of self and a secure environment to grow up in … We were very lucky!!!

Tensions and Resolutions

Life in Williamsburg was not bad—save for one episode that happened in 1954 when I was sixteen. After a couple of confrontations with the local Italian kids in the neighborhood over schoolyard playing turf and shouting matches in the local schoolyard, my mother took me off to Bermuda for the summer to cool things off. We stayed at a family friend's house; that friend had a travel agency, and he got me invited to a teenage party in the neighborhood. I walked into this party of strangers and sat around listening to songs like "I'm Forever Blowing Bubbles" and "My Little Red Top." It was a nice party, and the kids did make me feel comfortable. Around one or two o'clock in the morning, everyone started to get up and go home, so I started saying good-bye. A sweet-looking girl came over and asked me if I wasn't going along with them "to the sea," which was their term for the beach. I said that I didn't have a bathing suit, and she said, "You don't need one." We got into a pickup truck and drove toward what was called "Pink Beach," which was beautiful in the full moonlight.

During the ride, I had protested again that I did not have a bathing suit. They had all laughed and giggled. We got to the beach, and the game began. The boys were supposed to run as fast as they could, and the girls would chase them. What a nice game, since I could run very fast. I ran and was chased by a very fast girl. She caught up with me when I stumbled. She stood over me and suddenly took off her clothes, dripping water on my face and laughing. She said, "You're mine," and I laid on the ground with her enjoying Bermuda. I did not quite fully understand until later. I was profoundly introduced to seduction and sex on a lovely pink beach in Bermuda.

I did a lot of growing up on that island. I loved Bermuda. The people were so beautiful. The mixtures from Saint Davis Island in the northern part of the island, where the British naval base was located, were assortments of mulattoes and quadroons with blue and green eyes and with freckles and beautiful complexions. We drank ginger beer and went to the Cup Match between Somerset and St. George. This was my introduction to football (i.e., soccer).

I remember almost getting killed while driving a moped on the wrong side of the road and almost running into an oncoming lorry (truck), landing in a ditch beside the road. I remember walking along a beach skipping over the sand crabs on July 27, 1953; my mother yelled from the car that it had just been announced that the Korean War was over (which meant that Skippy, who was then nineteen years old, wouldn't be drafted). What a country.

I must have grown a lot taller on Bermuda because everyone remarked about how big I had become. In September of that year, the score with the local Italian boys who still held a grudge with me was "settled" meaning there would be no reprisals from the other gang members. I had another vocal confrontation with same group in the street returning from the movies at the Melba on Boston Road in the evening and said they want to fight only me. So my good friends Spence and Billy Brooks and Junius Chambers "held my coat"— and did not say "we got your back." I fought all five of them at once. I hit one square in the face, and he went down liked a sack. I hit another in the stomach, and he too went down like a sack. The other I kicked in the groin. They scattered and ran. The next day, I heard that the other Italian guys at Evander Childs High School told Skippy that I had put up a good fight and that it was over. I never had any other run-in with gangs or any groups after that.

I would like to mention a few other people that we knew in Williamsbridge in the forties and fifties. There were the older guys who lived on Paulding Avenue and 217th Street: the Mont brothers, Archie and Willie. Willy became one of the first black subway conductors for New York City and later became big in the union. Other guys were Richard Gibson, Chauncey, and the Ross Brothers, Edgar and Eddie. Handsome Eddie Ross later married his high school sweetheart, the beautiful Yvonne Cambridge. Other people on 217th Street were the Godfreys, fat Neil and his older sister, Barbara. Next to them lived skinny Lester Edwards. We have many pictures of the neighborhood kids: Howie Brown, Lenny Smith, Henry Perry, Richard Gibson, Herbie Seymour, Lovely Hill, the Thomas Girls, Rozella Lawrence, Jean Richards, Dorothy Brooks, Joan and Janet Fowler, and Phyliss Fowler. I tried to sneak into the great pictures they took at Riis Beach, scenes of the heroic boys and the fetching poses of the girls. One of those episodes was momentous because that was where Skippy met Anne Marie Richardson, his 1st wife and mother of his 2 children, Terry and Wendy.

Chapter Two

MY PARENTS

Mother Maude

My memories of my mother are very vivid—like cameos in a motion picture. Maude Atkinson Nichols was twenty-four years old when I was born. I noticed this when looking at my birth certificate. She was five feet five inches tall and was born in Sumter, South Carolina, on April 12, 1912. This was the date on her passport, but there was another date on her tombstone in the Woodlawn Cemetery—1911—and she told us still another date, 1915. So, what is one to believe? (It seems that both my mother and father had problems with their birth dates.) In fact I have heard this from many other people I have asked.

She was a beautiful, gracile, intelligent woman with very tiny feet. Her clothes, many of which were hand made, filled her closets along with her shoes, her long gloves, and her many hats—one for every occasion. Her many bottles of perfume and eau de toilette, of all different sizes and shapes, sat on her dressing table along with her glass Bambi powder container.

She attended Hunter College, but I don't think she graduated. Socially, she had many friends. The small house on Fish Avenue was often filled with ladies from the entertainment and education worlds. She knew the Brown Twins, Hilda and Vivian, and their brother, Louis, who danced at the Cotton Club[1] along with Cab Calloway and Lena Horne. She knew Nick Kenny of the Ink Spots, whom we visited in Queens, Mantan Morlan, Eddie Rochester, W. C. Handy, and his wife. She knew many Harlem socialites and members of several professional women's clubs, like the Girl Friends and the Links. She was very friendly with Freda De Knight from *Ebony* magazine and Helen Meade who was the director of the Little Brown Schoolhouse associated with the Hecksher Foundation. She had many clippings from the *Amsterdam News* that showed her attending parties and galas. She and my uncle Eddie knew Countee Cullen and other prominent artists in the Harlem of the thirties and forties. But my mother's life was not all fun and games. Langston Hughes's poem "Mother to Son" comes to mind. The mother tells her son,

> *Life for me ain't been no <u>crystal stair</u>.*
> *It's had <u>tacks in it</u>,*
> *And <u>splinters</u>*

My mother was a fortress to her children. She raised us alone for the most part. My father, who was a machinist, had two garages in the Bronx and Mount Vernon and was anxious to enlist in the army. He went into military service and overseas in 1942. Their correspondence attests to the difficulties that they had with mail and censorship. They separated soon after he came home on furlough in 1943. According to her letters, he had given her little support during that time, so my mother had to be both mother and father, making her the source of all discipline, which grew harder though appropriate with age. She was not squeamish about how she applied discipline to her young hellions; and in the end, when we were teenagers, she would chase us with broomsticks and dog leashes. She was ever vigilant about teaching us manners, and cursing was strictly taboo. She rigidly enforced all of this with icy stares of authority. "Mother Maude," as I called her when I

---

[1] The Cotton Club was built on the Northeast corner of 142nd and Lenox Avenue to compete with the very successful Renaissance Casinos, which was at 138th Street and Seventh Avenue. The Club was owned and operated by Owney Madden, a mobster and a bootlegger from Hell's Kitchen. The Cotton Club was famous for its major attraction, Cab Calloway, with his famous "Minnie the Moocher" routine.

was older, was not perfect. I must be fair here. She was not too much of a cook. Which demands a further explanation. Grandmother did not allow her gentle daughters in the kitchen. This was never explained to me, but it was obviously the truth. Consequently, Maude knew very well how to cook just a few things. Time was not in her favor, and she had to be very organized about preparing our meals. On Sunday, she spent the whole day cooking different meals. My mother was a great cook for those four or five dinners. The others were leftovers. This was our food for the entire week, which she put in plates or bowls for us, or if she was not too tired, for her to dish out and warm on a double boiler when we were hungry. She cooked her staples of chicken, macaroni, sweet potatoes, rice, jars of gravy, bowls of peas and carrots, and so on. This has made life difficult for our future wives. It has given me a chronic disease that I have had since childhood; I have had relapses and remissions throughout my life. It involves the dislike of, distaste for, and even refusal to eat leftovers. There must be a name for it.

Years later when my brother Skippy and I were having dinner at his home, somehow the discussion of eating leftovers came up. Shirin, Skippy's wife said, "Oh no—Leon [Skippy] doesn't eat leftovers. I have to cook fresh food for him." My wife, Gayle, howled with laughter. "Eddie never gets leftovers! I have to hide them as best I can if at all." I have had this conversation with other men that I have talked to at parties and in my office, and they had similar stories about their mothers, We lived in interesting times.

Mother lived from day to day for the most part—juggling bills and food ration cards, raising two hellions, and managing work. She had to be pleasant with Mike the butcher at the local A&P who always saved her a good selection of meat. I remember he would always give me a piece of bologna or salami. Like Dilsey, she endured. I remember her going to work every weekday morning—rain or shine, cold or warm—and returning at six fifteen by bus. I would meet her at the corner of Wilson Avenue and Boston Post Road and walk her home. I learned to have a stiff upper lip and hold my head high walking with her.

Mother's hectic schedule for survival left little time for levity or intellectual stimulation. She did however listen to her friend Helen

Meade who was a principal at the Hecksher Foundation and my third grade teacher Mrs. Mann who told her that she should buy me an encyclopedia. I treasured that big book. I read and memorized pages and pictures. I still remember the picture of the covered wagons being made in Conestoga Pa. from that exciting and revealing book.

Even though this is my memoir, it would not be complete if I did not include some thoughts that my brother, Leon (called Skippy), had about those early days. My brother Skippy, who is three years older than I am. remarked to me that "It would have been stupendous if we had a family that was involved in higher education, politics, the arts, literature, or business, any or some of these and who were friends and acquaintances with whom we could have heard interesting conversations and grew internally. We didn't even have a sense of humor, or laughter in our family. We didn't discuss anything." He went further, "I don't recall having any meaningful conversation with Mother except for arguments about money and her feelings about who we could associate with." I suppose she was too tired. If there were any discussions, they were brief and direct. On reflection, it was at those times I wished I had a father present to talk to.

My brother had strong opinions about our childhood. These feelings were later echoed by my Aunt May in long conversations about the family. There was never any emotion shown or spoken. No hugs, no kisses. Aunt May said that her older sister never played the big sister to her, never gave her advice, and offered no encouraging words. Aunt May said that Vivian Brown, whom we called Aunt Vi, taught her about lipstick and makeup and how to dress as a teenager. All this startled me. I had felt some of this coldness but never knew how deep and pervasive it was or how deeply it was felt by others. I felt as much love as was given. I knew nothing else. But Skippy and Aunt May were unanimous about the glum social life in the family, which according to Skippy was "an emotional desert."

I will go back to this topic in later chapters. It had great meaning in my later life in lessons I have learned and that I will elaborate on.

In the forties we were sent to summer camp in New York State, my aunt Helen's Craigmeade, starting in Craigsville and then finally in Roxbury, New York. Aunt Helen was a principal with the Hecksher Foundation and the Little Red Schoolhouse. She was also Skippy's godmother. Skippy told me recently that he had gone to camp from when he was eighteen months old until he was sixteen. There were four camps then. The first was in Belmar, New Jersey; the second one was at the Hecksher Foundation in New York. The third camp, which was the first camp that I attended, was a beautiful converted farm along Route 45 near Craigville, which is near Chester, New York, and had a big white house and two large barns on either side. The girls would sleep in the barn on the left, and the boys would sleep in the barn on the right. We were terrified by the holes and cracks in the old structure, which would probably be condemned under present rules. I remember Skippy having trouble with many junior thugs like the Albion brothers and Eddie Moore, whom Aunt Helen had rescued from the slums. I remember running into a barbed-wire fence and lacerating my ankle. More sutures and more scars were gotten in other years. We heard of VJ Day there in 1945, and we demanded that we be allowed to go home to celebrate. In fact a group of us were determined to walk home, and indeed we were allowed to walk until dark before we were picked up by "Uncle John" Mason an aide to Aunt Helen and driven back to camp. Another time we complained about the food and had to eat so many peanut butter sandwiches that we had stomachaches. There were two other counselors, Leon and Charmaine Pierre. Another counselor, Elvin, played taps. We sang the camp song.

> *We welcome you to Children's Village*
> *We're mighty glad you're here*
> *To keep the earth reverberation*
> *With a mighty cheer …*

Later the camp was moved to Roxbury, New York, the birthplace of the naturalist John Burroughs, who wrote "Wake-Robin," "Locusts and Wild Honey," and "The Breath of Life."

Aunt Helen's camp brought kids like me from the South Bronx into the countryside for eight weeks. The kids had to be disarmed and have their heads shaved. We were all given a tablespoon of castor oil followed by a wedge of orange on Saturdays. (I am still sickened to this day by the sight of a wedge of orange.) We had lots of adventures and experiences while at these camps. My main memory is of the many kerosene lamps that we had to use at night and the millions of moths that died in the flames. I also remember that we had to clean the soot from the glass chimneys. The third camp was spread over a slope on a large mountain. I remember "Uncle John" Mason, who was the camp driver and a very strong man. He would entertain and fascinate us with his feats of strength. He would hold a pair of twelve-pound sledgehammers at arm's length for a minute or two. He quickly established who was boss. We would go to the local dairy farms and milk cows and try to pitch hay. It was at Craigmeade that I tried to dive headfirst into a stream of water and cracked my head open and had to have sutures put in. I remember the spooky tales told by "Uncle Richard" Hackshaw, the counselor who took us on an overnight trip to a nearby field. We had to sleep next to the campfire wrapped in blankets, and we took the firestones out of the glowing fire for warmth. We saw the Milky Way and lots of shooting stars. We even saw the aurora borealis. I became a counselor when I was a teenager and was chastised by my plain-looking Aunt Helen when I complained that there were no "good-looking" girls my age at the camp. She said, "Beauty is skin deep, but ugly goes clear through to the bone."

My Grandmother

My grandmother, Sylvia Kershaw Atkinson Jackson, graduated from the South Carolina Colored Normal School in 1905 and then taught school in Sumter, South Carolina, at Morris College.

Sylvia Kershaw with diploma from South Carolina Colored Normal College1905

Sylvia Kershaw Jackson 1945

I owe much of what I know of her history to my Aunt May, who wrote the following:

> Sylvia K. Atkinson met Samuel Lewis Jackson in Orangeburg, S.C. Sylvia was on a lecture tour to raise money for Morris College (Baptist) which was supported by the Rockefeller Foundation. this meeting took place around 1926. I was with her. Maude was in the High school part of Morris College and Edward was attending the elementary school in the city. They apparently attracted each other to the point of corresponding regularly as Samuel lived in New York City. Samuel was a Stenographer typist on Ellis Island for the Immigration Dept. which in those days was a well paying and a prestigious one for a colored man. He later wrote a brief history called "Jackson's International Almanac, a pocket Encyclopedia of the Darker Races" which was published in the Vanguard Register on 2222 Eighth Avenue. He was helped by Uncle Eddie.
>
> Indeed, she ruled the roost at 750 Riverside Drive which my family owned at the time with its high ceilings and huge rooms. There was never any drinking, smoking swearing or anything going on in that apartment. This was all part of her strict Baptist upbringing. Her father was a Baptist minister whose parish in Sumter South Carolina is now supported as part of the United Negro College Fund.

Christina Saunders

Reverend Friday Kershaw

Her father, Friday Kershaw was a Fanti from Ghana, and the adopted son of Paul and Patsy Kershaw. Married a full blooded Cherokee Indian woman named Christina, the daughter of George Saunders and Isabelle James. Rev. Kershaw was involved in the building of Benedict College. i.e. he donated lumbar [*sic*] for the construction of the college.

Anyway, as I got even older, I never got a straight answer on some matters, like the question of who his parents were. I had virtually *no* information, *no* revelations about him, except that every year I would learn another family secret about life in South Carolina or how the family came to move up to New York in 1926. I found out that my grandmother's husband Edward Atkinson died of tuberculosis in 1926 and that she moved north with Samuel Jackson, who was a shorthand stenographer on Ellis Island. We would visit Grandma on Thanksgiving, and the apartment would be filled with the redolent smells of good Southern cooking—yams, collard greens with pig knuckle flavoring, sweet potatoes, Virginia ham, and corn bread

Samuel Jackson   Edward Atkinson

Aunt May, Uncle Eddie, Uncle Harry.

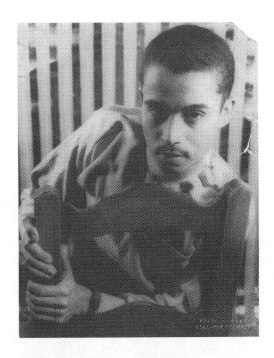

In answer to a letter that I had written to Aunt May in 1994, she wrote:

> Now let's see if I can do this very objectively (I hope).
> You know that that's the most difficult thing to do [is]
> write objectively about your family.
>
> Oakland Avenue, Sumter, SC the block I was born on
> in 1921. On one corner was a house inhabited with
> people I cannot even remember seeing or even heard
> their name. Next door to this house was one inhabited
> by the Sampson's. A nice family, husband and wife and I
> believe three children, one boy and two girls. The reason
> I remember them: Merriam their youngest daughter,
> who was a friend of my cousin Virginia. The house my
> grandfather owned and built, Susan Richardson, the
> youngest girl of the Kershaw's lived and died there.
> That was 215 Oakland. I was born, all of Ed Atkinson's
> children were born in 213, the house next door.
>
> My first memory was a kitchen momma was cooking
> breakfast (grits, gravy, bacon eggs and biscuits). It must
> have been on the Saturday, for that was the only time I
> can remember doing this. I was in the highchair, Maude
> and Edward [were] sitting at a small table (the kitchen
> wasn't that large) no conversation to my knowledge. I
> would look out on the back porch, it was on my right.
> They were two tubs, on I guess a stand. Maude was to
> do a wash. It mustve been a clear sunny day. Edward
> was not seemingly a part of this. As a matter of fact,
> once breakfast was finished, I supposed I was more or
> less on my own. Seemingly I was always on my own. No
> one as I remember talked to me. I would sit on the back
> steps busy doing something. I supposed looking toward
> the back of the yard, I remember seeing a small coop
> (chicken) in my grandfather's yard. The shed in our yard
> (wood) stacked high. I write this because in our adult
> years Edward always talked about some blocks he had
> inadvertently put in a hole in the side of the house under

the kitchen window and he never could get them out. This has always frustrated him (smile).

Maude was always a sweet sister and would do anything for Mama, Edward and me. I can never remember a harsh word, tantrum, temper, spoken in my presence. Edward was there, but not there if you know what I mean. Even on Sunday when we all went to church (Shiloh Baptist) a beautiful large church, Maude and Mama were members of the choir. Maude would sit in the rocking chair. I had a stool I would bring for her to comb my hair. The little pot belly stove was in the room(the main one where we always seem to be) moma's bedroom [was] right on the left as you enter the house. The bed was close to the window that overlooked the porch, I slept with her. I fell out of the bed many times, but never hurt myself. As Mama (she) kept enough space between the bed and the window for me to hit the floor without pain. Edward [junior] must have been there or maybe he was dressed and gone to Sunday school.

The next memory of my brother was a gentleness of always doing things to make me smile. Such as riding his bike with me on the handlebars to the creamery in town for ice cream. He never said anything but I always knew he was taking care of me. I felt so comfortable around him.

The years flew by, the next memory was in NYC at 26 Saint Nicholas Pl. Third floor front. A dining room, living room, two bedrooms, kitchen and a bath. We had a telephone (Bradhurst exchange or Audubon)on the dining room buffet. A Philco radio with Edward would always see that I heard Little orphan Annie and the Shadow knows. On Saint Nicholas place I looked out the window because 2 girls were calling out to Edward. I believe they were his classmates. Momma talked about it that night at the dinner table. (we always had dinner in the dining room when daddy Jackson came home from work (Ellis Island, he was a typist and a stenographer there.)). He (Daddy) at the head of the table, mama opposite, Maude on the other side, and me and Edward. When Maude married then Edward sat there. It was always pleasant there. Edward went to junior high school on 160 41 Edgecombe Ave. on 164th St. I went to PS 46 on 155th St. and St. Nicholas Avenue and then to Stitt (JHS164) and Ed graduated from the DeWitt Clinton H.S. and I got an academic diploma from George Washington high school in 1936(My heart breaks when I read about the decay of those two grand schools). Edward at Clinton was hit in the eye from a spit-ball and had to go to Presbyterian hospital for care. That was traumatic for me because he never complained. (By now we must have moved to 163rd st between Amsterdam and Edgecombe because Daddy had lost his (the Great Depression) and I'll go back for another incident (2 actually) that involved Eddie.

We lived on St Nicholas place. Eddie used to always take me to the playground on Amsterdam and 151st st (the Brown Twins's who lived in the apartment above us) was pushing me in a swing, I fell out and bruised both my knees (the scars are gone now, but they lasted for some time) Eddie carried me all the way home. Another time in the playground, some kid started a fight with Eddie. I remember (the only time I ever did this) jumping on one of them and bashing him back and wouldn't let go. Someone pulled me off and Eddie and I walked home. (Don't think we told mama) Also on St Nick I had the measles with high fever. Maude and I slept together, Eddie in the living room. Anyway, I remember in a haze, Eddie fanning me until I went to sleep. My favorite dolls' legs were broken. She always sat on a dolls rocking chair in the living room. Not sure about this, but someone fell over the doll and bother of her legs were broken. The next thing I remember, Eddie had plastered her legs back and painted them (brown) (she was a colored doll and gave her back to me without a word) I never knew he was doing this (so typical of him).

We lived at Macombs place (70) on the third floor. Eddie always saw to it that I had a decorated x-mas tree every year until I left for Finishing School and from there I married in 1942. He would buy the tree xmas eve night, guess it was because he can get it cheaper (I was supposed to be asleep when all was done, the decorating and presents) The next morning he'd come in the living room to see the presents, receive his, and that's about it. His 1st purchase when he got his 1st paycheck from the health department (1936?) was a Philco record player. He was so proud of it. All of us were. Eddie would listen for hours to classical records. He was well versed in the history of opera and the classics, and had quite a collection. I don't know what happened to it.

Ed was drafted for World War II. I do know he was very unhappy at boot camp. He'd write this to me, and happy day when he was honorably discharged. He was never a strong child or adult. As a matter of fact, on his 1st heart attack I went with him to the doctor (Montefiore Hospital) and he asked me if Ed ever had rheumatic fever.

He must have seen a defect even then. I remember he and Maude went to Europe together and he was very happy when he came back. He must have met Harry Brown during the war, as Harry was a veteran. Harry became his best friend and we automatically included Harry in our daily lives as brother, more or less. As Mama's health started deteriorating, Edward wanted to make her smile, and comfortable, as the colonial houses (a project) was fast becoming a slum. He thought that he could do this by purchasing 730 Riverside dr. He would tell us that the tenants were professionals and highly educated people, which they were, and momma would be happy there. The problems of being a landlord were overwhelming for someone as gentle as my brother. A gentleman should never become a owner of a building in new york city. He's too honest and truthfull. At about that time Mamma's health was very poor and the hardships of the building were too much for his heart. Harry Brown was very helpful to Ed at this time. Ed made him a partner, they stayed on the premises. Ed was a cracker jack book keeper. And he was paying back Ernst Tenes all of the money he borrowed when death struck. My brother was loved by everyone he met. This I know because I always hear from people in the health department that he was someone who always helped them and never forget their names ever. Even when he worked in the commissioners office, he would remember everyone of the personnel in the districts (clerical, doctors and nurses). He took a leave of absence and never returned. (now I know, he knew his heart was too weak) and that building was too much for him. Never complained though, always thinking of others. He was proud of Edward & Skippy who became doctors, and he loved Renae with all his heart. I hope they too when they think back will return that love to him and his memory. Oh I left out Rio DeGenero. Well, he had a studio condo on the copacabana, it was his. He went down there as often as he could. He looked forward to those times. Ed had some happy times, no more, no less than any of us.

I too have fond memories of my uncle Eddie (Edward Atkinson), whose name I share. He was a kind, shy, quiet, soft, and timid soul. He was given to listening to his classical music on his shortwave Panasonic radio, which got signals from all over the world. His library was filled with great classical books, including *Seven Pillars of Wisdom*, and books on philosophy and history. I never heard him speak above a whisper.

In fact, my brother reminded me that he rarely spoke at all. He would barely take notice of us, or say anything—profound or otherwise—to us. No advice, no thoughts or ideas. A photograph of him taken by Carl Van Vechten, the famous photographer and promoter, says everything about his personality.

He did, however, love his family, and he strived to help in any way he could. He took excellent care of his mother, especially in her dotage and senility. He provided her with shelter and care until her end when she succumbed to a relapse of tuberculosis, which had been the undoing of her husband when he was twenty-six. He had indeed bought the building at 730 Riverside to provide her with a regal abode, which he furnished with Brazilian chandeliers and mirrors. I heard stories from my other uncle, Leroy Stalnaker (May's husband), that he would have toga parties for his friends.

He loved to fly down to Rio de Janeiro where he had a condo that he rented to his political friends, who had to work in Brasilia, which at that time was being built as the capital of Brazil. Uncle Roy said he belonged to the Mattachine Society, reflecting his sexual preferences. He had told Skippy and me that the apartment building would be a sinecure for us in the future. I am also sure that he helped my mother finance my first years in medical school. Skippy told me of the family conferences that were involved. Incidentally, Skippy also told me that when he asked for financial assistance to go to medical school a few years later, Uncle Eddie refused to give him any money.

I was never aware that my uncle had cardiac problems. As was so common in my family, many things were not shared or addressed. Family secrets remained secret. I reread Aunt May's letter, and she even alluded to the lack of conversation at the dinner table. He did, however, once vaguely ask me what he should do about his difficulty walking up the hill at 152nd, where the apartment building was. I said after hearing this, "Do you have a doctor? You should consult him about your symptoms." It turns out that he never had a private internist or cardiologist and instead went to the VA Hospital for any emergency care. Sadly, he died in the VA Hospital in the Bronx where he had taken his life companion (Uncle Harry, who lived in the fashionable 409

Edgecomb apartments) for care. My aunt May called me, frantically telling me he had passed out on the floor during a massive heart attack. It was a sad end to a wonderful and caring uncle. He loved his mother and sisters and cared for them until he died. I wish I had known him better. He was so remote in his feelings. I guess he did not think some of his feelings would be acceptable in those times.

Skippy had lots of feelings about Uncle Eddie, and one day he will write them. But that will be his story.

My Father

The sad event of my uncle's death, led me to really wonder where he came from. What was his race? I frequently dreamed of finding my father. When I was an adult I did ask people, including my cousin Renae, to look for him when she was going to go to Washington and California to study. In the eighties—I do not remember exactly when—I did by some twist of fate get hold of a book called *The Wonderful Book of Nichols*. I have it somewhere. All of the addresses and telephone numbers of people named Nichols in the entire world were listed. And indeed I found the name Leon Nichols listed in the state of Washington on 1924 S. 331st Street, Apartment 103c, in Auburn, Washington 98003 (though I doubt it was the correct address). I did call that number, and a male voice answered the phone! I said jubilantly, "Hi, I am Edward Nichols. I have reason to believe that you might be my father." The man replied—and I quote—"No, that is impossible. I am German," and hung up. Naturally I was astonished; but nonetheless, I gave up thinking that the person I had spoken to was my father. How sad that I was mistaken.

So all of this leads me to discuss my father—my memories of him, the meaning of him in my life, the effect of his absence during my entire life, the effects of his absence on my profession, and how things developed and evolved in the search for my father over the past twenty years of my life. I will begin with what I knew about him and then move on to how I grew up and reached my goals. It has been a wonderful journey and story that is worth telling.

EDWARD A. NICHOLS, M.D.

Memories of My Father

Rudyard Kipling's poem "If" contains so many of the things I wish my father had said to me.

If—

by Rudyard Kipling 1865–1936

If you can keep your head when all about you
    Are losing theirs and blaming it on you,
If you can trust yourself when all men doubt you,
    But make allowance for their doubting too;
If you can wait and not be tired by waiting,
    Or being lied about, don't deal in lies,
Or being hated, don't give way to hating,
    And yet don't look too good, nor talk too wise:

If you can dream—and not make dreams your master;
    If you can think—and not make thoughts your
    aim;
If you can meet with Triumph and Disaster
    And treat those two impostors just the same;
If you can bear to hear the truth you've spoken
    Twisted by knaves to make a trap for fools,
Or watch the things you gave your life to, broken,
    And stoop and build 'em up with worn-out tools:

If you can make one heap of all your winnings
    And risk it on one turn of pitch-and-toss,
And lose, and start again at your beginnings
    And never breathe a word about your loss;
If you can force your heart and nerve and sinew
    To serve your turn long after they are gone,
And so hold on when there is nothing in you
    Except the Will which says to them: 'Hold on!'

If you can talk with crowds and keep your virtue,
Or walk with Kings—nor lose the common touch,
If neither foes nor loving friends can hurt you,
If all men count with you, but none too much;
If you can fill the unforgiving minute
With sixty seconds' worth of distance run,
Yours is the Earth and everything that's in it,
And—which is more—you'll be a Man, my son!

"Most American children suffer too much mother and too little father," observed the noted feminist Gloria Steinem in 1971. At the time I remember thinking how true that comment was for me, and had been all my life, especially when I was a child. I remembered, as a little boy growing up in the Williamsbridge section of the Bronx, New York, back in 1944, one of the very few occasions when I even saw my father; in fact I have no real memory of him until that time.

I have already wrote about the only large event that I remember about my father when he came home on furlough. I remarked how we were very insular in our community of Negro people.

In fact, we colored families were surrounded by the predominant mix of Jews, Italians, and Irish second-generation immigrants that made up the population of Williamsbridge. The Negroes were educated and very ambitious; there were many schoolteachers, lawyers, civil servants, store owners, nurses, and parole officers. There were no laborers or maids among us, nor anyone on welfare. At that time in New York, there were no Negroes, driving buses or trains; and there were very few colored policemen and no colored union workers. Working Negroes were not seen in the North Bronx when I was a boy. The two Negro policemen in the neighborhood, Mr. MacFadden and Mr. Lowe, worked in Harlem in the 135th Street precinct.

*I am an invisible man ... I am man of substance, of flesh and bone,
fiber and liquids—and I might even be said to possess a mind. I
am invisible, understand, simply because people refuse to see me.*
—Ralph Ellison, *The Invisible Man* (1952)

Despite the fact that my father was a light-skinned colored man and my mother, likewise, was what was often referred to as a "high yellow." We were still faced with the typical racist attitudes and reactions that were prevalent then, as now.

About my father there is very little to say or remember. I do remember his playing with us in the kitchen. When he came home the last time I saw him, he made "air pudding." He made big, sweeping motions in the air, making an imaginary pudding in the air and then putting it on a plate and giving it to us. I remember also his driving up Gun Hill Road with us in the back seat and letting the brakes slip while stopped at a light. We would scream with delight (or was it fear?). I also remember walking with him to the liquor store on Boston Road and smiling and laughing. I remember his being presented on stage in the auditorium of my school with his uniform and his medals. The fact that my father was never home, except during that one period, didn't trouble me when I was young. I accepted what was given. It was only later that I had questions and began to seek answers.

But there were other memories that I had blotted out, which came bursting out in my awareness. And so it began ...

The year 1943 and the first half of 1944 must have been very fragile years for my parents' relationship—at least if the letters he wrote are anything to judge by. But in August 1944, just before his short leave was over and he had to return to the army, I remember hearing a terrible argument between him and my mother one night. The yelling and crying went on for a while. It was hard to make out what they were fighting about, but I recall finally running into their bedroom to find my mother on the floor sobbing. My father had stormed out of the house. It was the last we would see of him.

My Father, as Later Learned, i.e. Another Redux

Before he enlisted in the army and became an engineer in the Army Transport Service and then held the rank of chief engineer on a ship,

Leon Nichols was a skilled car mechanic, He rented a garage on East Tremont and the Triangle Auto Service Company. My mother, Maude Atkinson Nichols, worked as a secretary to a colonel in the Army Ordnance Department, which was a few blocks away from my father's garage.

Despite that terrible night in August 1944, when Leon Nichols walked out forever, my own, albeit vague, impression of my father was that he was a warm, sensitive man who loved and lived for his wife and sons. Therefore, I never understood or knew why mother severed her relationship with him. My sense of who he was and how he felt about his family was borne out by the letters we found fifty years after the fact. But that is another chapter in our lives that I will discuss in later chapters.

My family decided after my graduation from PS 78 in the Bronx that I would attend DeWitt Clinton High School. My uncle had attended Clinton many years before, so it was sort of a tradition. Besides, my brother did not want me tagging along at Evander High School where he thought he was king. In any event, I took the 15A bus from Wilson Avenue and Boston Post Road to the 206th Street station, transferred to the 15 bus to Mosholu Parkway, and then walked down to the high school. The principal, Mr. Walter "Crazy Legs" Degnan, ran a tight ship and was the coach of the football team, he used the players as stair guards. The guys on the football team were huge and fearsome and had won a lot of city championships.

I have never had too many memories of De Witt Clinton except that I had some great and memorable teachers, especially the large brunette Spanish language teacher, Sra. Maria Emilia Colon y Pico de Moscoso, who made it a point to tell us that her name wasn't *Mocosa*, which meant "fly." She liked me and wrote in my yearbook "*Todo tiene su fini,(bueno o malo) Me alegre de, por fin, hayas aterminado bien sus estudios.*"- translation: Everything has an end, (good or bad) I'm happy that you did well with your studies. I also remember Mr. Archie M. Cushing, who taught French. I was put in the writing class of the school paper the *Magpie* (with Mrs. M. Whalen) and remember that Richard Kravitz and Henry "Hank" Coshburn were in the same class. We would meet later in our professional and social lives. Richard trained with me in pediatrics at Montefiore Hospital, and Henry became a vice president of an oil firm. Somehow, I was able to win a place on the track team at the high school (probably from running away from my brother) as well as the cross-country team—and won my letter C for the sport, which I still have. There were not many other extracurricular activities available because most of us didn't live close by and had to catch a bus or a train right after school. I must have missed a whole lot of the fun that other people enjoyed in high school. I will never know. I went to summer school at William Howard Taft, taking additional courses and gaining another semester before graduating. I was three years ahead of the classmates my age. How and why I did that still remains a mystery. But therein lies another story.

It has occurred to me that the reason I went to DeWitt Clinton High School in the first place was simply that my uncle Eddie had gone there and my family thought it better for me to go there because of its high academic standards.

There are two other reasons that come to me as well. The first is that I could never have gone to the same school as my brother (who was three years older) because we would have been in the same grade. The dire ramifications of that would have been innumerable. Second, I would have been extremely distracted in classes with pupils three years older than me—especially in a coeducational school.

Chapter Three

GROWING UP AND BUSTING LOOSE

College

One of the biggest disappointments as I look back on my college days is that I had no guidance from counselors about what courses to take and what degree to go for. I didn't have a clue as to which courses to take; I only knew I wanted to be a doctor, so my premed courses were thrown at me. I remember the first day of registration in the main hall; one of the large lecture halls inside contained listings of all the classes that were available. All you had to do was make a schedule for about ten courses that would be enough for matriculation in the semester. Before you could make complete sense out of it, someone would come along and erase or cross out one of the courses you intended to take, so you would have to start over again. Naturally, the best professors were taken before I got a chance to sign up, and most of the other students were eighteen or so and had some prior knowledge—but I had no clue.

I remember attending the classes in biology and chemistry and having the feeling of despair. There were very few people who would help other students, and most people would try to hurt. And I will never forgive the administration of City College for the fact that there was no guidance counselor to help me. Now, mind you, in order to get into the City College of New York, you had to have a better than a B-plus average; but being fifteen and without a clue should have garnered a little assistance. I took courses in calculus and chemistry, which I hadn't the faintest idea about or understanding of. I never understood what mathematics was about from the start. Whether that was a matter of nurture or nature was debatable. The guidance counselors gave no guidance. I was a minnow in a big ocean filled with sharks that chased me for grades.

I thought because I wanted to be a doctor of medicine that I would have to earn a BS, with a premed major. I did not understand that I could have gotten a BA and minored in premed courses. I missed out on such great courses in literature, composition, and debate. Instead I took calculus and physics and organic chemistry. Good grief! I discovered my misunderstanding later when talking to friends who had gone to Harvard and Yale. Carter Marshal, who attended Harvard, earned a BA in history and English, and minored in premed. He got fine grades, as did John Norton at Columbia. Later I found out that my daughter Christiana also earned a BA and minored in premed. I did manage to take German, which I loved and which suited me well later in my studies.

I was also in the ROTC. Imagine the reaction of the battle-hardened Southern sergeants who were the teachers of this short (five foot seven) fifteen-year-old with braces to my becoming a second lieutenant in the regular army on graduation. I was a social misfit. All the other students were three or four years older. There were still older veterans who were premed students. They looked at me in amazement and disbelief—if not disdain—and gave me every D they could. We drilled in the cavernous Army Hall and the stadium. Diana Lorieo, a classmate of mine then, and a lifelong "member" of the family, reminded me that Colin Powell was in the ROTC at the same time and was even in the elite Pershing Rifle Drill Team. I vaguely remember that there was a study hall in the basement. A hole in the wall called George's Men Shop was later expanded to Sir George Limited on Broadway at 113th Street and served Columbia students. We studied in the basement of Findley Hall. I don't recall all the courses I took but was reminded again that we took speech classes in Army Hall including courses in general debate, exposition, and extemporaneous speech.

Diana even reminded me of the CCNY school song ("Sturdy sons of City College, Trusty hearts …") and the school colors, lavender and black, all of which had escaped in the bottomless pit of lost memories. I remember walking through Shepard Hall (the main building) and Harris and Baskerville Halls and wandering around the newly opened Manhattanville South Campus, a property measuring eighteen and one-half acres (and which had previously been a convent) that extended from 130th Street to 135th Street between St. Nicholas Terrace and Convent Avenue.

I remember especially "the five neo-English Gothic buildings which were terra-cotta and stone. They were built in 1907 and the grounds of the old Convent and Academy of the Sacred Heart. And the Greek amphitheatre of Lewisohn stadium donated by Adolph Lewisohn." (These details are from *Wikipedia*.)

Some, not all, of the black (then called "Negro" or "colored") students spent their free time in the cafeteria playing bid whist. Most of the black students were from West Indian families who lived in Brooklyn and Queens, like Wilma Murray and Marie Henry from Brooklyn, There were very few American Negro students like Leo Samuels from Morningside Avenue and David Single from West 150th Street. Many Negro students sat together, separate from the white students, who were mainly Jews, also from the Bronx and lower Manhattan. Many of the older Negro Americans were veterans of the Korean War and were much older than the average students. The few I remember were Calvin Cunningham and Roy Innes. Of special mention were Lolita (Lolly) Forde and her brother Kenneth Avril Forde, who were from Barbados. Other students worth mentioning at the time were Howard Brown, Lorne Bristo, Calvin Simmons, and Dagny Lohar.

This was the time of the CCNY point shaving scandal (1950). This was the also time of the Yippies, with their pseudo communistic pretensions and frequent, noisy but useless anti capitalistic demonstrations. I did make friends with two Cuban American families whose families had been kicked out of Cuba by Fulgencio Batista. I do remember the handsome Barnabe (Berney) Loreto DeMola from Forest Hills, Queens, and Maria (whose last name I can't recall). They were also in the Caduceus Society. On reflection I remember Prof. Dawson and Prof.

Sayles in the Biology Department. I also remember the comparative anatomy professor, Dr. Fahrquar. He asked one day if I thought that my age had any influence on my poor grade average. At least he was curious about my feelings. He later tragically committed suicide.

Diana Canales reminded me during our long musing about CCNY nostalgia that we had taken German together with a Prof. Mierman who was the epitome of the bald Prussian pedant who hated women and all minorities. I do remember his constant drills of the accusative and dative (*durch, fuer, gegen, ohne, um, wieder, nach, zeit, von, zu*) and a phrase from the book we were translating Die Erste Aufuerliche Kuende uber di Germanen, haben wir von Tacitus. During this time, I read lots of books by Dostoyevsky, Tolstoy, Cicero, and Plutarch as part of the curriculum at the college. After all, this was the home of intellectualism and political science. This was the home of the Young Progressives. (Yes, there were many Communists studying there.) I have learned since graduation and conversations in the decades since that many of the Jewish students had scripta of the lectures and access to most of the exams that were given. None of these ever came into my hands. I learned this from the Jewish students who went to med school in Basel.

I do remember that I would go across the Jasper Oval, where students played handball, basketball, and so on, to meet friends who were my own age and attended the High School of Music and Arts—friends like Billy Brooks, whose classmate Billy Dee Williams was in our group. It was in that group that I met Joan Hughes who, unbeknownst to her, had entirely and innocently contributed to my becoming a man. Less innocent were my encounters as a seventeen-year-old with Anita Nelson, the tall blonde gal in my economics class who wore black leather pants and jacket and drove me on her Harley-Davidson to her apartment in the East village for tutoring lessons.

At Lewisohn Stadium there were concerts by the New York Philharmonic and the Metropolitan Opera and even Duke Ellington during the summer; ROTC drills were conducted there as well. I remember one year when I had partied for several days on the weekend at the Penn Relays in Philadelphia and had drill in the early morning hours. I was at parade dress when I asked the person standing next to me, "Why is it getting so cloudy all of a sudden?" The next thing I knew, I was flat on my back staring up at several very concerned cadets and officers. I hadn't eaten much in the last few days and evidently had a hypoglycemic episode. I had to borrow money for breakfast and recovered after a Danish and coffee.

These were nevertheless exciting years that molded my character. During this time I naturally had to find my way socially, to extend, to develop. Friends my age were still in high school. We were just getting to seek out and talk to girls.

There were rounds of parties at the different Jack and Jill affairs. There were the Christmas parties. There were three or four circles of friends, and the Manhattan Jack and Jill organization, the Brooklyn crowd of the Centurions, the Bronx crowd in the Bridge (i.e., the Williamsbridge section where we lived), and the Mount Vernon crowd. A few words about the Mount Vernon Crowd: As with all of these groups, we gravitated to them because the people were the same color and financial class that we were, and were social isolates like we were. They became an extended family. I am not sure how we met them. Skippy had met them also, and we boys had met a younger group. All of us came to know each other and still hold close ties. The main family groups and individuals were the Richardsons, the Potters, the Tarters, Richard Gibson, Herbie Seymour, the (Orris) Powells, Sabra and Eddie and the Andersons, and the Nashes. We later met the Careys. The Williamsbridge kids included the Lowes, Jackie Sams, and the Fowler girls, Joan and Phyllis.

Other wonderful girls from the South Bronx were the Owens girls, Marcia and Yvonne. I would visit them in the early evening riding the "El" to 168th Street and walking (and eventually running later in the night) to the train. Yvonne was the older sister; she wore fashionable clothing that was quite alluring. They had a little brother, Jimmy, who later became a virtuoso jazz musician. Jackie Stewart was a beautiful brown-skinned girl who had such an athletic body and a great sense of humor. She later became a phys ed instructor at some university in Massachusetts. We played at life and romance but, as with most, lost contact. Perhaps I will find her one day on Facebook.

We extended our network beyond Williamsbridge by word of mouth and the telephone. I am sure that my friends Billy Brooks and Junius Chambers and my next-door neighbor Basil Thomas knew more about the social network than I did. We got to know girls and boys on Sugar Hill and even in Brooklyn. They were mostly connected with the Jack and Jill organization. At any rate, we went to parties in the homes and community rooms of apartment buildings and got to know the different crowds of people we would know for the rest of out lives. I have often said in later years that the people you meet between the ages of fifteen and twenty-five, you will know and run into for the rest of your lives. The kids we got to meet were mostly fair-skinned and children of professional parents. This included the teachers, civil servants, and small business men. Everyone thought they were well-off or at least certainly not poor. There were a scattering of dark brown children (and their parents were certainly moneyed by way of medicine, or funeral home or liquor store ownership) in the crowd, but for the most part the children were light brown or very fair.

The Brooklyn crowd centered around the Centurions, Roger Bennett, Roger Whitehead, Billy Pickens, Stuart Taylor, Warren Goins, Christopher Chisholm, E. T. Williams, Conrad Pope, Tony Johnson, Phil Taylor, Mike Henningberg and their girlfriends Janet Martin, Alma Arrington, Marilyn Whiting, Marilyn Warner, Gayle Yancey, Faith Sherman, and Donna Mayer.

I graduated from CCNY in June 1956 and was in a dilemma about going to medical school. When I was eighteen years old and a senior at CCNY, I sought the advice of one of my girlfriends—the pampered, oversexed, extremely yellow Cheryl Wormely at Sarah Lawrence—to try to get into Howard University Medical School. I eventually went down to Washington, DC, to talk to her mother, Margaret Just Butcher, a prominent though eccentric English professor and the author of *The Negro in American Culture*. She was the daughter of Ernest Everett Just. She told me candidly that my chances of getting into Howard Medical School were slim to none. My age was the main obstacle; the fact that the school had a regional mandate to accept students from the South, along with my B+ average, would mitigate against an early acceptance. I was dismayed and disappointed.

Back in New York, I sought the advice of another girlfriend and asked her father what I should do. Dr. John Moseley, a graduate of Harvard University and then a radiologist at the Mt. Sinai Hospital Center, advised me to go to Europe for medical school. I had studied German and French in college and high school, which would surely be a help to me. He suggested I go to some medical school in Europe for a year and then into Tufts University Medial School in Boston. Dr. Moseley continued to be an inspiration to me my whole life, and I am greatly indebted to him for his encouragement and direction. He always found time to talk to me when I visited his beautiful daughter at the elegant Roger Morris Apartments at 555 Edgecombe Avenue on Sugar Hill in Harlem. I was amazed and grateful for his help when I needed guidance.

I had to prepare myself to ask my mother about the prospect of going to Europe. All those moments of reflection, which seemed like hours, broke me out in chills. But I finally went to her while she was combing her long hair at her dressing table; I told her that I had spoken to Dr. Moseley and that he had said it would be great and that he could get me into Tufts and all. There was a moment of silence, which seemed like minutes. Then I remember her turning to look at me and saying, "Why not!" I was shocked. I don't remember if I collapsed, sighed, or just stood there dumbfounded. It was the best news I had ever heard. I think she was overjoyed also. It was only later that I learned there had been a lot of family thought about my going to school in Europe. Finances were discussed at length with the family. My brother told me this at length years later.

My mother had had the good fortune of going to Europe with her brother, my uncle Eddie, in the spring of 1950. She went on a shopping tour in Paris that was financed by *Ebony* magazine because she had done a three-page spread for the fashion section. She and Uncle Eddie visited Switzerland and took tours in Zurich. That was a wonderful trip for her, but it also opened the doors to Europe for me in years to come.

Mark Twain wrote in his essay "The Turning-Point of My Life" that "the turning point … is only the last link in a very long chain of turning points commissioned to produce the cardinal result." Twain tells his readers that Caesar urged, "Let us go wither the omens of the gods and the iniquity of our enemies call up. The die is cast."

There are many links to my going to Europe to study medicine. There were, however, no doctors in my family, no dreadful diseases overcome, no outstanding scientific discoveries I longed to discover, Mostly it was the desire to be the best that I could be, and that was beyond any doubt to be a doctor of medicine.

In conclusion one might say that I was neither well born nor well bred. There was so much indifference, My big chances would come later.

Chapter Four
MEDICAL SCHOOL IN GERMANY AND SWITZERLAND

I shall be telling this with a sigh
Somewhere ages and ages hence:
Two roads diverged in a wood, and I—
I took the one less traveled by,
And that has made all the difference.

—Robert Frost

I mentioned before that I had a working knowledge of both French and German from studying both in high school and college. So I applied and amazingly was accepted to the Faculté de médicin at the Sorbonne in Paris and the Johannes Gutenberg University in Mainz. I talked with my mother, and she talked to the family; and one fine afternoon she told me that the family would finance my going to Europe to study medicine.

I left the wonderful borough of the Bronx in October 1956. I sailed aboard the SS *America* bound for Le Havre. What a crossing! We ate in grand style in large dining rooms—three or four meals a day served at tables with stewards! We ate fine foods, and red and white wine was served. I roamed all over the ship, including into first class. The stewards knew my mother's boyfriend, Sy MacArthur, so they kept an avuncular eye on me so that I wouldn't get into any trouble. Two days out we ran into a huge storm that raged for two days; the boat pitched and rolled dreadfully. I went outside near the stern and hung on to the ropes and staggered to the rail and watched the surging wrathful sea throw Italian marbled waves over the bow. Everyone except me and a few others was horribly seasick. I was often the only passenger in the dining room. I ate heartily (no leftovers), watching the rolling of the boat darken at first the starboard and then the port side portholes. It never affected my appetite; I was still growing.

This was my first taste of elegance and the good life. I was in heaven. I met other students on board and slept in the same cabin with French and German boys returning from their own American adventures. I tried my small German and French vocabularies and was happy when they responded in their language and didn't laugh at me. More happiness. I also found out about the French and German senses of humor. The French understand nuance and the pun. The Germans have no sense of humor.

Arrival at the port of Le Havre was an adventure in itself. My French roommate and companion, another student, invited me on deck, and with a wave of his arm he shouted, "Voila! La France!" He was so proud. I was equally surprised to see a black gendarme on the pier walking up and down guarding his country!

I had intended to enroll at the Faculté de médicine of the Université de Paris but was advised by a beautiful colored girl named Marie Claire (whose address I was given by my mother) that I should go to school somewhere in Germany. I decided after talking to other medical students in Paris that it would be too difficult to start at the Sorbonne. The exams were written in French, and they marked against mistakes in French!

It was interesting how I came into contact with Marie Claire in Paris. All I was given was her address in the Rue du Grenelle. I found that the Rue du Grenelle was located on the Left Bank (Rive Gauche) and was extremely long. In any event, as I was walking along the Rue du Grenelle, I saw two German girls (well, two girls speaking German).

Since I spoke German better that I spoke French I approached them and asked them for their help. Amazingly enough, they actually knew her! They did! Isn't that fate? Marie Claire was pleased to meet me. Her mother had told me I would be seeking her out. She laughed at how the gals I had encountered actually knew her. Marie Claire was so kind and understanding, or as they say in French *sympathique*. We discussed life among the clochards on the banks of the Seine, and she wisely said that I should leave France and study in Germany. Perhaps she noticed how bad my French was and how I would suffer with the Parisian professors.

"EINIGKEIT UND RECHT UND FREIHEIT"
German National Anthem

Einigkeit und Recht und Freiheit	Unity and justice and freedom
Für das deutsche Vaterland!	For the German Fatherland!
Danach lasst uns alle streben	For these let us all strive
Brüderlich mit Herz und Hand!	Brotherly with heart and hand!
Einigkeit und Recht und Freiheit	Unity and justice and freedom
Sind des Glückes Unterpfand;	Are the pledge of fortune;
|: Blüh' im Glanze dieses Glückes,	|: Flourish in this fortune's glory,
Blühe, deutsches Vaterland! :|	Flourish, German Fatherland! :|

wikepedia

I therefore decided to matriculate in Mainz in October 1956. I spent a semester there learning more German and then transferred to the University of Basel in Switzerland for the next five years.

The University of Mainz is situated on a large hill overlooking the old city of Mainz. The city is famous as the home of the invention of the movable-type printing press; the first books printed using movable type were manufactured in Mainz by Gutenberg in the early 1450s. During World War II, more than thirty air raids destroyed about 80 percent of the city center, including most of the historic buildings.

The school was used as a military school for German officers during WWII. There were many *hakenkreuze* (swastikas) painted and etched

51

in stone all over the walls and ceilings of the school buildings. The dormitories were cold and austere, and the halls were dreadfully dark and full of echoes—at least they were that night when I arrived at eleven o'clock. The foreign students were not allowed to speak in their native languages, and most of the students except the many Persians spoke German all the time.

At the University of Mainz in West Germany I was introduced to the spartan rigors of German university education. Again only German was spoken, which was hard but absolutely indispensable for learning German. Mainz at the time was still a town of rubble since the end of WWII. Mainz had been in the French zone of occupation, and there had not been any agreement with the French to rebuild the city. The Germans however were quick to remind them that Germany was the home of German culture and science. Mainz University was called Johannes Gutenberg University after the inventor of the printing press. And it was the home of the Max Planck Institute of Nuclear Science. The German professors and students always reminded the foreign students of the cultural history of German. We learned of the medical history of Germany and were exposed to the music of Brahms, Beethoven, and Haydn all the time. It was a cultural awakening for me. I did remember music appreciation in elementary school and my cranky, stern music teacher, Mrs. C. Jereme, playing the records and talking to us; but here I was at the source. It was fascinating.

I learned most of my German in the Katakombe, which was a cabaret in the cellar of a bombed-out building in the old city. The Katakombe had a theater in which the poet and actor Hanns Dieter Hüsch gave performances, including pantomimes. I soon learned there are differences in what is called humor. The Germans have a different humor, which is schadenfreude (slapstick or pie in the face). I learned to speak very quickly from two sinuous, tall, blond German sisters, named appropriately Renata and Inge. They taught me a lot about Germany. Those are unforgettable memories—my first encounters with lust and romance. I met them several years later in Frankfurt at the medical school and hospital where Renata had become an assistant professor of medicine. There were many other foreign students at the university who were studying medicine. I met Sudanese and Coptic Christian

Egyptians and four West Indians from the New York area and two others from Trinidad. Percival Pottinger, Gums, and Felix are the names I remember. Dr. Gums now lives and works in New York and plans to retire in Saint Martin where many Dr. Gums live.

I was also fascinated to see brown children walking with German women. These were the children of the liaisons between the African and American Negro troops during the occupation. The children's hair was long, worn in what would now be called Afros. The women had no idea how to comb or brush their hair.

I stayed at Mainz for one semester taking lecture courses in the premed sciences. More of my mother's friends or distant acquaintances (she had many) lived in nearby Frankfurt. I would visit them on weekends. One wonderful man, who worked for the European Recovery Program in Frankfurt, advised me to transfer out of Mainz and go to a Swiss school. I remember as if it were yesterday my riding back to the Frankfurt Hauptbahnhof and seeing a neon sign for Basler Versicherung (Basel Insurance); I said to myself, "I will go there to look at the medical school." On the man's advice I went south to Switzerland and arrived at Basel on a cold, bright day in April. Switzerland was incredibly different from Germany. It was like night and day. Whereas Mainz and even parts of Frankfurt were cities of rubble and despair, Basel was clean, prosperous, and healthy looking. They drove Chevrolets! (I later found out Chevrolet was originally a Swiss auto company.) There were beautiful homes and chalets with flowerpots filled with geraniums in the windows. There was no dirt or litter in the streets. There was no crime! This was the home of fondue, birkemuesli, and chocolate!

Circumstance is man's master—and when
Circumstance commands, he must obey.

Circumstance is powerful, but it cannot work alone; it has to
have a partner. Its partner is man's temperament—his natural
disposition ... It is born in him, and he has no authority over
it ... Nothing can change it, nothing can modify it.
—Mark Twain, "The Turning-Point of My Life"

TRITT INS MORGENROT DAHER
National Anthem of Switzerland

When the morning skies grow red,
and over us their radiance shed
Thou, O Lord, appeareth in their light
when the alps glow bright with splendor,
pray to God, to Him surrender
for you feel and understand
that He dwelleth in this land.

Before talking about my stay in Switzerland, I want to discuss what I will call the leitmotif of my sojourn in Europe. It was more of the same preoccupation with culture and history of Switzerland and the Swiss. They are fiercely proud of their unique history and culture.

I was happy to apply to the medical faculty of the University of Basel. The university was famous in Europe and had been established in 1462. The famous Paracelsus once taught anatomy there. Since I had some time before my appointment to speak to the dean of admission, I had the sense to go to the art museum (the Kunstmuseum), which I had heard so much about while preparing to go to Switzerland. I saw the works of the Holbeins, Rodin, Calder, and other artists in the great halls of the museum. Later when I went to speak to the dean, he asked me what my impressions of Switzerland were, and I told him that I had been to the Kunstmuseum that morning. He was astonished, to say the least.

Matriculating in medical school

I gamely asked to speak to the dean, Prof. Bernard, and was ushered into his office. I was amazed to hear the odd German he spoke. It was as if he were speaking to a child using the diminutives. This was Swiss German, which is called Schweizerdeutsch. She was very surprised to hear me speak German so well. His secretary remarked when going into Professor Bernard's office, "*Der Neger hier spricht Deutsch!*" He came out expecting a wonder! indeed, we chatted for a while. He was interested to know what I thought of Switzerland. I told him that I had only been there for a few hours and that I had been to the art museum. He was shocked by that response. He accepted my application and told me to return in the afternoon because he was having a committee meeting after which he could tell me if I had been accepted or not. I was flabbergasted. This was all serendipity. Everything was working out so much better than I had expected.

I remembered that I had known a guy, Arthur Goldberg, who had graduated with me from CCNY and was in Basel at the medical school; so I called him, and we went to lunch at the rooftop restaurant of a department store called Globus. It was a small version of Macy's or Bloomingdale's in New York. What a contrast between this and Germany. Arthur was surprised that Professor Bernard had been so friendly and accommodating; he and his friends had had quite a hard time getting accepted. There were several other Americans eating in the restaurant who were older army veterans, and I later found out were also students on the GI Bill. I had somehow stumbled upon the place where many Americans who had not gotten into medical school in the States had found a medical school where they could become doctors. Most were American Jews, and most were from New York. These were guys who were as determined as I was to become a doctor. I knew I was in the right place.

Well, after lunch and a brief tour around the city. I went back to see the dean. Imagine my surprise when he told me that I had been accepted for the next semester. It was a dream come true.

An Aside about My Personality

By temperament I was often the kind of person that does things—does them and reflects afterward. I had to learn to reflect *prior* to doing things. I was a work in progress. I was young, and my mind was absorbing incredible amounts every single day.

I was never diffident. In fact many called me arrogant. I would say I was justifiably proud.

My Thoughts on Basel and Switzerland

I would like to add here my thoughts about the city, country, and people I have come to love.

When I arrived in Switzerland from Mainz in the spring of 1957, the contrast with postwar Germany was striking. There were beautiful houses with geraniums in the window flower boxes, which contrasted starkly with the rubble and decay that were the legacies in Germany of the Second World War. Red-cheeked boys and girls ran through the streets in Switzerland, while German cities seemed nearly under populated with children. What a country—an abundance of everything, proud and confident. The exchange rate of the dollar to the franc was in my favor—nearly five to the dollar. This made it possible to survive on my pitiful loan from the state of New York.

No city in the world except New York has ever changed my life and outlook as Basel[2] did. The city of Basel lies on the Rhine River at the corners of France and Germany. Basel is an ancient city, first developed by the Romans, which is now a commercial center noted for pharmaceuticals and clothing manufacturing. The population then was certainly smaller than the 170,635 inhabitants in 2012.

---

[2]   The city is divided by the Rhine into Grossbasel to the north and Kleinbasel to the south. The two sides are united by the bridges. Outstanding works by Hans Holbein the elder and younger, Conrad Witz, Klee, and Calder are shown in the permanent collection of the Basel Kunstmuseum.

"The University of Basel was founded in connection with the Council of Basel. The deed of foundation was given in the form of a papal bull by Pope Pius II on November 12, 1459, and was known throughout the history of Basel especially with the presence of Erasmus of Rotterdam during the Reformation. It is famous for its anatomy museum, which has the collections of the early anatomists such as His and Langerhans. Other scientists associated with the university include Paracelsus, Daniel Bernoulli, Jacob Burckhardt, Leonhard Euler, Friedrich Nietzsche, Eugen Huber, Carl Jung, and Karl Barth" (Wikipedia).

Switzerland lies in the Alps

Often, while staring at the pictures in my office, I will see a picture or map of Switzerland and Basel, where I studied so many years ago. I remember clearly all the adventures and gatherings we had some fifty years ago. We had beer and wurst in the Barfüsser sidewalk café on the Barfüsserplatz in the center of Basel, where all the streetcars would rumble through and where we often met in the nice spring and fall days after class. Later we met in the *kunsthalle* where the clique had a *stammtisch*; the group included Benno Nussbammer, Kiep Fessler, Rudolph (Rudel) Reber, Freddie Blattner, and Peter Plattner. We would meet on Saturdays at five or six to plan the weekend social events. We would also discuss the world and its problems and also ogle the pretty girls passing by. Now I look back at those times and think of them as tall Hobbits sitting around the large circular table and spinning tales of foreign travel and latest loves. We drank beer and smoked lots of cigarettes. I felt proud to be included among the guys.

Only one woman was allowed to sit with us—the witty, charming, and willowy Lislott Egeler, who was Christoph Egeler's younger sister. (I will have much more to say about the Egelers.) Women were usually not allowed at those meetings. They would, however, meet us later to go to the other gatherings or parties. Girlfriends included the tall, thin, beautiful Verena Kellerhals and the taller and more beautiful Lilliane Erzberger and of course Bea Meidinger (how smart!) and the short, cute Sonja Hunziger and the unforgettable Margrit Speich (who held my hand walking through Basel).

We knew many other students from other universities, including Mumsie Widmer, Hagen, and many others. They were a happy band of friends, driving around town with their Vespas, the current rage at that time. My old friends still send me postcards of the places they visit where we had once been. I remember the times we had raclette or fondue in some chalet restaurant or at someone's house. In the winter, especially after Christmas, we went to ski resorts in the high Alps in Zermatt and Davos. I remember also our trips to Rome and Paris in the spring. My dear friend Sammy, whom I will write about in later chapters, would look at each of us and say, "Imagine all that for poor boys from the

Bronx." We'd take trips to Zurich on the weekends to go to the student parties. At one of those parties I met Christoph, U. P. Meidinger, and the lovely and mysterious Nicci von Kanitz. Sammy and I kept saying, "This is wonderful!" Quite a change from Williamsbridge in the Bronx. It was indeed different. I felt sort of like Dorothy when she entered Oz; we weren't in Kansas anymore.

But I am getting ahead of the story—the pace at which it was happening was so fast and furious.

As one can imagine, my first years in medical school were difficult. Getting used to speaking German, especially speaking and understanding Swiss German, was difficult. The lectures were in High German, but the people spoke Schweizerdeutsch, which was a strange dialect and difficult for Germans to understand. The different professors came from different cantons of Switzerland and had different accents. I did not know many other students and had to study hard to get into the swing of things.

My first years were spent in preparation for the arduous first examination the Propädeutikum, which determined if you would get into the final three-year program of the clinical years. The classes included physiology, biochemistry, anatomy, and histology. It took a little time to get used to studying in German and learning the technical work, but over the next two years, after many hours cloistered in the small room that I had rented, I was prepared and passed my second-year exams. I remember being very lonely in my one-room apartment on the Nonnenweg 9, heating it with briquettes of coal that cost twenty-five centimes and putting *zehen rappen* called *zehnerlis* in the meter to get hot water for a bath. I remember lighting what would later become my famous candle and melting wax on it until it grew into the phallic 4 foot tall monstrosity that I still have somewhere in the basement.

I was alone for the most part, and in the first two years of medical school I corresponded with my girlfriends in New York. Bernadette Carey wrote often of her cub reporter days at the *Washington Post* and her dates with David Frost and dinner at the Stork Club and Twenty-One. I didn't hear any more from my old friend Jane Moseley who had been at school in Mexico. She went on to marry Joe Hoffman, who graduated from Harvard. I am sure her mother and father were pleased with such a fine guy. (I met Joe later in life, and indeed he is a fine man.) They had a lovely daughter, Cathy. Unfortunately, they were divorced six year later. She explained to me later that the average marriage lasts seven years; I wonder where she got her statistics. I got encouraging letters from other girls like Rosemary Irving and Claudia Burkhart from when they were in college. They have remained friends for life.

I dreaded going home to New York in the summers. There was always the constant hint of an idle threat: that there would not be any financial assistance available to return to school. I did mange to take out a New York Higher Education Loan to guarantee my return.

In the second year of my stay in Switzerland I met the young Liz Campbell whose father was E. Simms Campbell, the cartoonist who created *The Sultan* in *Esquire*, and *Cuties* in the *Journal American*. They lived in Herrliberg, a suburb of Zurich. Liz and I met a small group of Swiss and other foreigners at a great party given by her voluptuous fellow student at the Art and Theater School of Zurich, Francoise Trudel. It was there that I met Christoph Egeler and U. P. Meidinger from Basel. They were students at the Eidgenössische Technische Hochschule (ETH; Federal Institute of Technology). Also attending the ETH was an attractive—in fact, beautiful—Swedish girl, Katerina Huberta Graefin von Kanitz. She and her sister were quite an attraction at the party. In fact Nicci (that was her nickname) and I developed a strong friendship, and I started dating her regularly—but that is for another chapter.

I was also happy that Sammy Mac Fadden came to study in Basel. He and I had grown up in the Bronx, and we had both been mentored by Dr. John Moseley (indeed I spoke to my dear and good friend John Norton recently at Martha's Vineyard, and he told me he had also had long conversations about medicine with Dr. Moseley). Sammy had taken the same good advice and started medical school in the spring of 1959. It was certainly nice to talk to someone from home. Being away from the family for such a long time can be difficult.

Sammy and I grew up together in Williamsbridge. I wrote to him when I started in Basel, and he came two years later. It was nice to have him with me in Basel. He was a great friend and had an infectious personality. We were a social success with that gang. They really took us under their wing. The Swiss are notably xenophobic, but we witnessed none of that.

Christoph's family lived in his father's house in Binningen, a lovely suburb of Basel in the half-canton of Basel Land. The house (better described as a chalet) was an enormous two-story affair with five bedrooms upstairs and lots of room for gathering and discussion in the huge dining and living areas. Outside were a pool and a lawn with nice tables and chairs and of course an area for playing boccia. Herr and Frau Egeler were then in their late forties and didn't mind our presence. Herr Egeler had a construction firm operating in the city specializing in renovating old—I mean very old—houses and buildings in Basel. He did the city hall and even the city opera house. The family is related to the Swiss painter Arp and the engineers that were involved in the construction of the George Washington Bridge. Christoph's brothers and three sisters were very young at that time: skinny Lislott; young, cute Katherine; pretty Suzanne; and red-cheeked, smiling Martin. I am truly blessed to have known them for the last forty-six years and still am in contact with them. We shared lots of experiences in our youth; for example, we went tobogganing in the nearby hills, tying four and five sleds together and slicing down the steep slopes like lunatics, laughing and screaming with joy.

Before leaving this chapter I would like to add the names of a few of the other students who kept us all alive and happy: the Norwegians, Carl Erik Schultz and Molfried Moulag; the Persian, Abul Hamid Sheiksadeh; the Hungarians, Ferenc Follath and Andras Horvath; the other Swiss, Felix Harder; the Spanish guy, Emilio Del Pozo, and the Indian, Gopinath Naia.

But my five years spent in medical school were not always so arduous. During spring and summer vacations, I hitchhiked with friends from Basel to Oslo or even Naples, often with a beautiful German girlfriend, Traute Sturm, and in the process learned much about the people and culture of Europe and about myself. I was introduced to the poems of Rilke and Heine. Another student from the Ukraine, Ella Kresnobayeva, taught me words and phrases of Russian and urged me to read more of Gogol, Tolstoy, and Pushkin. All of these adventures were stories in themselves. I spent two weeks in Vienna and strolled around the beautiful Schoenbrunn Palace and the Prater, a park with a giant Ferris wheel, and the Vienna woods in the suburbs and the magnificent Ring of Vienna. I stumbled on a huge stable with its wonderful smells and saw beautiful white horses being trained. They were the famous Lipizzaner Stallions. Who knew? I went to the Borg Theater to see magnificent productions. It was amazing. I imagined how Mark Twain must have felt when he watched the Imperial Parade of the Austrian Emperor. The streets were so grand and impressive. Everything was spectacular to my young and inquisitive eyes. Can you imagine operas in Basel and Vienna, cabarets in Mainz and Berlin? It was all mind-blowing. I felt so alive in Europe, so young, so aware of the new world whirling about me. The colors were so bright, the music so clear. The prose was so intense, so full of meaning. I was in the midst of youth and living every moment as best I could. I was not prepared to counter the Europeans with our American culture. I was not aware of the impact of American culture on the Europeans. I was not aware of how impressed they were with American jazz. They were so knowledgeable and fascinated—especially in the French cantons of Montreux and Luzern. There were many American jazz musicians coming through Basel, playing in the clubs and the casinos. I even went to a Count Basie concert in Zurich.

Here I must mention one of the most exciting times I had during this time, in the second year of my European education.

There was an International Exposition in Brussels in 1958, and Sammy and I really wanted to go. Luckily, we were in contact with Bennie Primm, who was studying in Geneva. (He had been a sergeant in the army and was wounded when parachuting. He maintained his papers to get into the PX's and bought cigarettes, and sundries and sold them in Switzerland. He used that money to rent apartments and sublet the apartments to other students. He made enough to live large and drive a car.) Bernie volunteered to take us with him to Brussels. In other words, he was a mover and shaker even then. I will always admire him. It was a magnificent event. Brussels is a wondrous city. But the big moment of the Exposition was the Russian exhibition of Sputnik. The world marveled at the Russian adventure into space. We met four or five Africans from what was then the Belgian Congo; they were students at the university. One of them, Justin Mboko, and I met later in New York when he became the foreign minister of the New Republic of Congo. Bennie and Sammy and I had a great time at the Exposition. Bennie graduated from the University of Geneva and later became a huge director of drug clinics in New York. He was on the president's advisory board. I wish I knew more about him. We walked along the Avenues of the Exhibits with our mouths open, gasping at all the new stuff. We were astonished by the Soviet exhibit, which had models of its newly launched *Sputnik* satellites, including a flight that carried a dog named Laika[3] (although the United States had launched its own successful satellite, *Explorer*, in 1958).

---

[3]   Featured at the Brussels Expo in 1958 was the Atomium, a futuristic building that represented an iron crystal magnified 165 billion times and that highlighted the positive side of the atomic age. The Atomium produced five tons of chocolate each day of the Exposition. The Brussels Expo was perhaps the best-known international exhibition during the Cold War period. As the first one held after World War II, it acquired broader significance: the governments of the European Western Allies—France and Britain—used the occasion to demonstrate their postwar successes. However, the theme of the US exhibit, "Unfinished Business," dealt with, among other subjects, America's social issues, including segregation. (Southern congressmen took offense and cut the remaining US exhibition budget. As a result, the number of US scientific exhibits were reduced, and Russia took over the unused US space in the International Hall of Science, using it to good effect as a propaganda showcase of Soviet technological advances; it had, for example, a display on the peaceful uses of atomic energy by the Soviets.) There were a variety of scientific products demonstrated, including an audio encyclopedia, an electronic dictionary, pasteurized cheese, magnetic tape capable of transmitting millions of characters in a few seconds, and a postal machine that could sort a thousand checks in fifteen minutes.

Chapter Five

NICCI

In my second year at the University in Basel, things blossomed socially. I have written how I knew the Egeler and his noble band of friends, but I must share here how I came to know him. When I came back from vacation at home in the Bronx, I was given the address of a colored family who had a daughter that I did not know from the Jack and Jill days but whom I was willing to meet. E. Simms Campbell lived in a small hillside villa on the outskirts of Zurich on the lake of Zurich at Seestrass 35 in Herrliberg. He was an émigré artist like James Baldwin; he had left New York, where he has been a friend of Gordon Parks, and settled in Switzerland, where he continued cartooning for *Esquire* magazine (*The Sultan*) and the *Journal American* (*Cuties*). He had a young daughter, Liz, who was seventeen and awkward, but also cute and very pleasant.

I was invited to visit and received a very strange welcome. E. Simms was an alcoholic's alcoholic. He was hardly ever sober. After profuse hellos and hugs from the family, he showed me his well-stocked wine cellar, gave me the keys to the house, pressed 100 Swiss francs into my hand, and told me, "Take good care of my daughter for the weekend." I was flabbergasted! She was a nice-looking girl, but I thought she was just a kid. What was he thinking? We did go out together after that, and I met her girlfriends at the Art and Theater School in Zurich. One weekend, one of her school friends—a buxom, blond Alsatian (named appropriately, Francoise Trudel)—who was very beautiful and very oversexed gave a party. The party was incredible. There were about twenty people there—young, groomed, cultivated, intelligent, and from all over the world. I met Sam Eldin from Egypt, Hans and Greta Chi from Luzern, Christoph Egeler (the only Swiss there, I might add), and two lovely, quiet, shy Swedish girls from Zurich. This party changed my life. The Swiss guy turned out to be a lifelong friend, and I married one of the Swedish girls.

Nicci (or rather Katherina Huberta Gräfin (Countess) von Kanitz) was born in Leobschutz in Pommern (Pomerania), which is now Poland, on September 22, 1939, the daughter of Ursula Grafin (Countess) von Kanitz and Ultz Graf (Count) von Kanitz. The family has long and deep roots in the history of both Sweden and Germany, and I will not bore you with all that right now. The family moved—or rather escaped—to Switzerland as a result of World War II in order to recover the money that Ultz's father had cleverly left in the country. It seems he divided his assets in thirds in Switzerland, Germany, and the United States. The money he deposited in the United States was confiscated as part of the 1945 reparation act, and the assets in Germany were lost to reparation, so the family lived on what was left in the accounts in Switzerland—and they have lived on this money for the last sixty years!

I had no idea of all this but was fascinated by the Greta Garbo aspect of the two sisters when I met them at Francoise's party and was indeed first attracted to Monika, the older sister. We went out on two occasions, but there was never anything there. I went home the next summer and received a letter from the younger sister, Nicci, inviting me on my return to come down to Ticino in the Italian part of Switzerland along with the Swiss guy from Basel, Christopher Egeler. Of course I said yes, and when I returned to Basel Christoph (or "Stoffel," as he was called) took the train to Locarno into a fantasyland that exist forever on earth. We traveled through the massive St. Gotthard Pass, which then required the transfer of the cars to a train and which took a very long time to traverse. (Since 1980 a ten-mile tunnel has been opened, which cuts the travel to about three and a half hours from Basel to Lugano depending on the traffic jams at the tunnel entrance.)

As an aside I must add the following tale. When I returned home to the Bronx after three years, most of the girls I knew, including Jane and Bernadette, were already betrothed or even married. I had little opportunity to see anyone, being without funds (i.e., broke) at home. I worked as an extern at Montefiore and one summer at Bellevue Hospital. I had absolutely, no social life. In a sense I felt abandoned by those girls whom I had such strong feelings for. I had little opportunity to meet or go out with anyone else. Any chance for a social life came from Europe, and I was heartened that Nicci von Kanitz had written to invite Christoph and me to come to Locarno to see her father's new home in the lovely mountain village of Ascona above Locarno in the Tessin in Switzerland.

We traveled south through Luzern down through the Massif Central's St. Gotthard Pass between Goeschenen and Airola; then we passengers had to transfer to a special train through the steep, winding turns, which took about two hours. I was always looking out for the beautiful church in Hospental, which we passed 3 times on different sides before reaching the long passage south. Locarno is a small town on the northern rim of the Lago Maggiore in the canton of Tessin (Ticino in Italian). While the people spoke Lombardian Italian, they were Swiss and fiercely proud of it. Swiss flags abounded in public and private buildings. We were astonished by the pristine beauty of the place. It is a spectacular scene to behold, both day or night. The center of town has beautiful arcades with lovely shops and boutiques, and the city rises into the mountains along winding roads. The chalets and homes were built on the mountainside in an sweeping arc along the lakeside coast. The chalets were all decorated with geraniums or ivy and had small balconies and shuttered windows. They were huge, often with two sections—one for the animals and another for family living. Most were single, but there were also some gorgeous apartments that were built along the winding roads toward Orselina, some four miles up the slopes that end in the Cardada.

When we arrived, we were met by the girls and went straight to their lovely home on the side of the mountain, a six-bedroom villa called La Vignetta (the Vineyard). It was beyond my comprehension, being a poor colored boy from the Bronx. The Villa had a lovely balcony with a stupendous view of the Lago Maggiore, with the far-stretching Maggia Valley rimmed by huge snowcapped mountains. What a place! We were told to get ready for the party, which was to be held at a new house that they had built, which had been designed by the famous Italian architect Visconti. We drove in the Volkswagens, further up on the hillside above Locarno, to the small village of Ascona, and there on the edge was a small road that snaked up onto a dirt road to a large house nestled in the woods.

The house was like no house that I had ever seen before. The windows were huge, twenty feet across and eight feet high, overlooking the valley, which could be seen beyond the tall pine trees below. Overhead there was a funicular to the ski slopes of the Cardada. The house had many strange angles and doors, something only a wild man—doubtless an Italian—could think up. The buffet offered many strange and wonderful things to eat like shark's back and truffles, which were served by cute little blond and brunette, sexily frocked waitresses whom I wanted to pinch. Lots of different French and Italian wines were poured as well. What a place! I was in another world—a veritable fantasyland! But I thought lots of Switzerland seemed unreal. We spent a wonderful weekend there and somehow returned via the St. Gotthard Tunnel to Basel, my head swimming with memories.

Nicci invited me to visit her in Zurich, where she was studying engineering at the ETH—the MIT of Switzerland. Christoph Egeler also attended that prestigious institute. In the ensuing months of 1957, we had great weekends together. The loneliness of the first year in Basel was over. I had arrived in a new home in old Europa. Nicci and her sister Monika filled my days with culture and finesse. I learned how to eat artichokes and drink sherry, to go to concerts and plays in Zurich. What a paradise!

There is a movie called *Bread and Chocolate* about an Italian worker who goes to Switzerland and sees how beautiful everything is and how primitive he is—that was about how I felt then.

Nicci showed me a whole new world. We went to cultural events, plays, art galleries, and concerts. Nicci, who was so interested in art, introduced me to the works of Calder, Klee, Arp, Alberto Giacometti, and the architect Le Corbusier. In fact her sister Monika's boyfriend and future husband, Sergio Salvioni, collected Giacometti works in his home. She taught me what and how to eat the delicacies that were so plentiful in Switzerland. She and a life for me were in Europe. We were in love.

Once Nicci and I fell in love we could not be apart. She came to Hamburg where I had an externship and continued her studies as a lab technician there. When I held a clerkship in Paris she joined me there. I was not alone and felt much better. As my time abroad grew shorter I began to worry, as a diary entry from that time attests:

> I think of her too much and realize this can only be bad for me. Thoughts of separation constantly haunt me. Our life is doomed, that is certain. I can't let her go. Tears come to my eyes when I even think about it. I hope that something miraculous would happen to save our happiness. I leave it up to the Gods!

I had no premonitions of the future, nor omens to predict my fate. I was living day to day. Remember that I had been through the ordeal of a rigorous one-and-a-half-year study period as a candidate for the final *Staatsexamen* (the national state boards) and the ORAL exam, which lasted six months and covered twenty-four subjects in German; then came my internship which had me working every other night. Nicci and I had been through many periods of separation before. Once before, while I was in Paris, she had called me saying that she missed me so much and needed to be near me. She came to visit me while I was doing a *stage* (an externship at various hospitals) and living in the Maison des États-Unis in the Cité Universitaire. She immediately got very passionate, and we made love. I soon felt and discovered a mass in her lower abdomen which led me think that she had an enlarged uterus, and then she told me that she was two months pregnant. She had never told that she had missed any periods. We were alone and frantic in Paris, wrestling with the question of what we should do. We did think about the possibility of my stopping my studies and us getting married, but we both thought that would be crazy since I would have no prospects for the future without continuing my education. Finally after failed gestures at an abortion in Catholic France, where it was forbidden, we called her mother Ursula who, thank God, saved the situation by arranging for Nicci to have an abortion in Zurich. I left my internship at the Hôpital des Infantes-Malade and accompanied her to Zurich. After the abortion I had to leave early to get back to my internship, and Nicci was furious that I abandoned her. The chief of pediatrics, Dr. Catela (from Marseilles), was also furious that I took off from the *stage*. I told him I had to take care of a personal problem, and he called me a liar—*un menteuse*.

We never had long, deep talks about living in the US or even getting married. We did think—and assumed—we would one day get married. But like most people, we never considered the consequences. We never—or, at least, I never—had concerns about her being white and my being colored. I had no idea there were so-called miscegenation laws in several Southern and Western States. I had no way of explaining things that I did not understand. I wanted to continue my professional education and had no idea how difficult it would be for her to adjust. Our young student lives were spent in Europe where it was less of a concern. I am sure her family might have expressed their concerns about her marrying someone who was not of their social milieu or race, but they never expressed their concerns to me or confronted me. Ursula always said, "Water seeks its own level."

Nicci came to live with me in Basel, which was so comforting to me during my preparation for the upcoming Staatsexamen. She started training in the Frauen-Spital as a venipuncturist. We kept house for that year and a half. I finally had regular meals and company.

Bodanas

No chapter about Nicci would be complete without my talking about Bodanas. Bodanas was an estate in Nässjö in the province of Småland, a vast area covered with lakes large and small and huge forests of tall pine trees. The estate covered six hundred acres and had a big private lake on the property along with a large country home with an old wooden annex that had beautiful old tapestries in its large rooms.

I was obliged to sleep in the annex because of bed space. It had also been used as a summer cottage by Catherine, queen of Sweden. It had brocaded walls picturing the bygone age of the eighteenth century. There was also an outhouse that I had to become familiar with. But because of what I was reading, I remember the boathouse where there was a Mangel,(a device to press clothes) which impressed me. I have never heard of one but I learned what it was used for by the staff that maintained the residence.

I loved the big dinner we had with Ulf and Monika, and *froken the family maid. "Froken" means girl.* serving the prawns. We drank aquavit and beer chasers, getting drunk, and then had fish and meat. The brave of us then ran to the lake and jumped in naked. What fun !, what Joy!. Ah youth!

Chapter Six
THE STAATSEXAMEN

The final exam, called the Staatsexamen (or national boards), was arduous and long. We had finished two years in the clinical years of studies and prepared for the exam for six long months. I studied every day in the university library: forty-minute sessions with fifteen-minute breaks. Each evening I joined three Swiss students—Maurus Vogel, Elisabeth Studer, and Isabelle Renggli—to review lecture notes and test each other with sample questions. We even had some of the frequent exam questions of the different professors. Our oral examinations covered twenty-four subjects we'd studied in the six-month semester. We were summoned by letter to the Wildt'sches Haus on separate occasions. The Wildt'sches Haus was a large patrician house on Petersplatz on the opposite side of the university buildings, where many official gatherings and concerts were given.

Three professors questioned each of us for an hour. Many failed. Somehow I survived. It was a horrible, exhausting process. At the end, I felt a heady admixture of pride, relief, and thanks. We were given our diplomas by the president of the Examination Commission, Dr. Vischer, who, incidentally, was a pediatrician.

I'd always wanted to be a pediatrician, somehow caring for children; through some Freudian or Jungian thought process, the ghost of my lost father and the need for a caring family might have played a role. This is where the "Physician, heal thyself" theme comes into play. I know that after fifty years, I still enjoy being a pediatrician and nurturing and helping to mold the lives of future generations.

I thoroughly enjoyed the diagnosis and treatment of infants and children. I envisioned myself doing important research at the National Institutes of Health or the Centers for the Disease Control of Children and finding cures for many pediatric diseases. I wanted to be like Jonas Salk.

Professor Doctor Med Adolf Hottinger

I was taught pediatric medicine from lectures given by my professor, Dr. Adolf Hottinger, who had been a student of Prof. Guido Fanconi at the University of Zurich. I enjoyed going on rounds with him, and he took a liking to me also. He was so influential in my becoming a pediatrician. I wrote my doctor's thesis on Thalassemia minor under his guidance and tutelage.

The final two years of medical school were quite arduous. Each week we were called on to practice in front of hundreds of students. We answered questions until our professors were satisfied with our performance. Some professors were quite disagreeable and submitted us to their ego trips. A particular professor, Rintelen, who taught ophthalmology, once stormed into the lecture hall screaming, "Where are the Americans? Stand up!" We all grudgingly rose.

He yelled, "No—not you, Nichols! I was at the concert"—his voice was getting louder—"and didn't see any of you ... except him, this *Neger* [i.e., Negro]. Imagine, this Negro," he said, pointing at me. "The rest of you are a culture-less rabble—*ein kulturloses pack von Ratten.*"

Everyone shuddered in silence when he allowed them to sit down.

I am proud to have been taught by such great doctors. There were other equally good doctors that deserve mention. In internal medicine Professor Staub taught us how the think analytically about the diagnosis and treatment of patients. He was a stern teacher and would counter when we gave incorrect answers by asking. "Why is that not at all correct?" We spent many chilling lectures and much laboratory time in pathology and histopathology, which were taught by Professors Werthemann and Scheidegger, and forensic medicine with Professor Im Obersteg, who would fascinate us with current coroners' cases from the city that were brought in. Professor Schuppli taught us dermatology. Professor Koller in ob-gyn had a son who was in our class. Professor Kielholz taught psychiatry. All these names bring back so many memories of the clinical years of my studies. They also bring to mind another student friend, Milo Zachmann, who kept up our friendship until his early death. He too, became a pediatrician and kept in touch even when I was in the army.

Maurus Vogel's reflections of the times.

In the following section, Maurus shares thoughts about that time.

Before that, we only knew of dark people from magazines and films of missionaries and the derogatory appraisal of these people, as you must have painfully heard from Prof. Rintelen. And that the Catholic prince of Monaco will absolutely have a white successor, even though he has already produced a black young man. Now, Obama becoming the first black president was indeed a gigantic event. And perhaps then soon a black Pope who will not only be pious but will have an attitude of "yes we can."

I remember that in 1960–1962 in the clinical division of the woman's hospital the [mostly uneducated] women refused to have a Black "Neger" person examine them. That was the Zeitgeist of the time. Now things are much better but not entirely as there are still some restrictions you can read from my last letter.

Maurus sent me this in February 2013 in response to my request. I was made aware that there was a problem with the Swiss women in the Frauen-Spital clinic (the woman's hospital) not wanting to be examined by black student doctors. I wonder if that was explained to the white Students. All I remember was that we were also taught using "phantom" devices to simulate a women introitus (in the vaginal area). I found all this unscrupulous on the part of the university, but they were all subject to the times.

We not only had Prof. Rintelen in Basel but also the great Prof. Wolf-Heidegger in anatomy and a world-famous professor of surgery, Prof. Rudolf Nissen. Nissen served in the First World War as a medic and was wounded (shot in the chest). He studied medicine and trained as assistant to Prof. Sauerbruch in Berlin—but then had to leave Germany because he was Jewish. He became chief of surgery in Istanbul and then, after the beginning of the Second World War, emigrated to the USA, where he had to repeat his residencies and licensing examinations. He was active as chief of the surgical division in Boston from 1941 until 1952 and then director of surgery at the Jewish Hospital of Brooklyn and Maimonides Medical Center in New York City. In 1952 he was called to Basel to serve as a professor of surgery, which he did until 1967. He developed many new surgical procedures, including fundoplication of the esophagus, wrote many books, and received many honors.

The president of the Examination Board was Dr. Vischer, a pediatrician. He belonged to the old blue blood elite of Basel and was responsible for giving us the final grades and diplomas.

Maurus sent me a letter dated Saturday, March 9, 2013, in which he shared additional details. I have loosely translated this correspondence below.

Dear Eddie,

I struggled a lot to refresh my memories of our State Boards. I have already talked about Prof. Staub and Nissen. An important man was Prof. Staub in internal medicine, a grumbling "Berner who spoke terrible high German. Having to appear with him in the lecture auditorium would make our hearts pound. A wrong answer would provoke a response question of "Why is that not at all correct?" He had the great ability to teach us analytic thinking and to narrow all the many symptoms of a patient into the most probable cause. Other main courses were pathology and Histopathology. It was an incredible amount of knowledge. There was also Prof. Werthemann, an eloquent, friendly typical Basler and the dry Prof. "Sigi" Scheidegger. In dermatology, we had Prof. Schuppli a typical officer type. It was funny for a dermatologist to have the name Schueppli, because the word means "flaky" and describes dandruff. In legal medicine Prof. Im Obersteg was a glistening figure. When there was a crime in Basel his lecture was at that time completely filled. In pediatrics, I remember Prof. Hottinger and ask myself if you, in your training, were influenced to be a pediatrician or if there were other motivations. About Prof. Koller I remember above all his hoarse voice and his son Teddy, who studied with us. I believe he married Marlene Brenk and was always preferred by all the other professors. In psychiatry we had Prof. Kielholz, who was such a young, rassuger [sympsthetic] man, with a dry humor, and Prof. Dukor ("Duki"), who was like his psychiatric patients. His son also studied with us and later married the blond, Steffi Obrist who drove her new VW. She became a psychiatrist, and he a pediatric surgeon and practiced in Vienna. He died recently from cancer. Occasionally we had lectures in neurosurgery from Prof. Klingler, who wore many colorful ties, which made him stand out. We also had a Hungarian professor of hygiene, Prof. Tomcsik. Prof. Luescher in ENT (Ear Nose & throat) impressed me later on, since he personally instructed us in the fine points and beauty of ear lavage, an activity that I have often used in my practice. I hope that I have inspired some memories and you can pick out some useful remembrances.

Maurus closes with Hearty greetings from me. Looking forward to mentioning of your biography in the yearly alumni publication Alumni Basilensis.

Chapter Seven

TRANSITION TO NEW YORK:1962–1969

After five and a half years of study, I passed my final exams at the University of Basel in Switzerland and became a doctor of medicine. I had prepared for one whole year, studying eight hours a day—both alone and with my study group of four. The exam itself took three months to complete, twenty-four exams in all, including internal medicine, surgery, pediatrics, and forensic medicine. I studied in the university library for seven hours and later joined my good friend Maurus Vogel, who was Swiss, in Reinach, a suburb of Basel, and I studied with two ladies, Margaret Studer and Isabelle Renggli. Every evening we prepped each other for the different exams. It was a grueling experience, endured with so much work and patience.

I still remember the exams and the professors. I still have dreams of taking the exams, of answering questions entirely in German. I leaped for joy. Many times, I wrote my name, followed by MD or beginning with "Dr." I called home and told my mother that all of her sacrifice, money, and time had paid off. Maurus and I celebrated with all the others, hugging and kissing our colleagues, drinking lots of beer, laughing, crying and yelling, shouting and cheering. I remembered all the great times I had enjoyed in Basel, a city of some 250,000 then, with a two-thousand-year history of culture and development, a city where I met lifelong friends like Christoph and Vreni Egeler, Urs Peter

Meidinger, Felix Harder, Ferrenc Follath, and others. From there, I had hitchhiked all over Europe, seeing England, France Norway, Sweden, Spain, Italy, Austria, Holland, and Belgium during the semester breaks, soaking up the history and culture of Western Europe. I had met and fallen in love with Nicci von Kanitz and was soon destined to marry her in Locarno.

These were truly life-changing times. I had been away from America and read about what was going on in *Time* and *Newsweek*, which came out on Wednesdays. Of course I read the international edition of the *New York Herald Tribune* everyday. There was so much going on, but I was paying more attention to my preparation for the oral exams and had little time to reflect. I had been thrilled at Kennedy being elected years before, and I avidly followed what had been written in the press about the days of Camelot. I was indeed distracted by the civil rights movement and lamented with Maurus about the problem of discrimination. He barely knew what I was talking about but bravely said. "You don't have this racism here in Switzerland." I could share that feeling.

This was a time of great civil unrest in the United States. There was a great awakening of Negroes. In fact there was confusion about what name to use—colored, Negro, Afro-American, African American—which changed every two years and went on for decades. And then finally came the notion that "black is beautiful." This caused lots of discussion and argument among blacks of different hues. Most of my friends were light-skinned, if not nearly totally white, but had been raised as black. When I came back to the US in the late fifties "Black is beautiful" was the rage. This did not sit well with our light-skinned parents, who were in their fifties and sixties and set in their ways. My friend Gilly Anderson, who was clearly white, had fallen in love with a beautiful colored girl in Brooklyn and brought her home several times. His mother was quoted as saying, "I brought you three steps forward, and you are bringing us two steps backward."

All of these racial issues about race, class, or color played out socially at the Jack and Jill club parties that we went to. The same questions always came up: *What does your father do? Where are you people from? Is he a doctor, lawyer, teacher, or what?* I told the story of my father, which had been embellished to say that he had served in the navy as an officer, aboard a PT boat, and was wounded when the boat was torpedoed, after which he received a medal. He had come home to see us when I was in 3A and presented to the school as a hero on stage. I had been so proud of him then. But he had left us soon after that, disappearing from my life. I could not say he was still in the navy and the war had been over for years. Mother had a good job with the IRS. That was the story, and I was sticking to it. I am sure others thought what they would, but no one questioned me further. I would not know the real version until much later in my life.

In Switzerland with Maurus, however, he and I argued about the Swiss Army. He thought the army was very powerful, and from his perspective it was. I had to get the dig in that the Swiss Army could not beat the Bronx National Guard. Naturally that stoked the embers of his Swiss pride to a hot fire and led to further heated discussions. Apparently Switzerland, like the rest of Europe, was in a big recession, and the dollar exchanged for four Swiss francs, which allowed me to eke out subsistence with my New York State loan. Maurus would come back with "Well, the *kaufwert* [buying power] was only 2:1." I could only think that I could buy a lunch and dinner for either 35 cents and the deluxe dinner for 3.75 francs (75 cents). Maurus, like most other Swiss would, always came back with "Europe has so much culture— Bach, Beethoven, Mozart—what do you have?" I answered, "We have European culture, but we also have jazz and bebop, the blues, Duke Ellington, Count Basie, Stan Getz. We have baseball, football." They barely knew what I was talking about.

Maurus and Christoph both came to New Rochelle to visit in the 1980s. We have been in letter contact for the last fifteen years since the Internet allows quicker contact. How would I describe Maurus?. He was—and is still—eloquent in German, either spoken or written, suave, and a *charmeur*. He uses his shih tzu as a woman trap on holidays in the South of France, where we have met on holidays in May. He loves to cook extraordinary meals and definitely likes to drink different wines and liqueurs. I have learned much about the different apertifs and digestifs from him over the years. Christoph Egeler was always a rake, flirtatious with all the young girls who passed his way. He had a smirk of confidence and drove his wife Vreni crazy. He is gallant and brave. When I visited him in Tuscany some years ago, we went to the Adriatic Coast, where he went windsurfing in spite of having had a triple bypass years earlier. He has been a very good and faithful friend. Pretty Vreni, like Penelope, has endured all of Christoph's antics since we were young.

I should add here the anecdote of meeting Christoph's mother at a masked ball in Basel's city opera during Fastnacht. This witch appeared suddenly before me and started shrieking about things I could not imagine she could know. I've been afraid of people in masks since I was a kid, but this witch really frightened me. I screamed, "Get away, you witch!" It was Frau Egeler, doing what Swiss women do at Fastnacht. I don't think she ever forgave me. One day I will tell Christoph or his sister Lislott this story.

The Swiss had been very nice to me. I had been invited to their homes, enjoyed dinners with their families, celebrated holidays with them, and gone on great skiing trips to Davos and Zermatt. No, things were quite different in Switzerland. I was told by many friends and even professors to stay in Basel and continue my training. As much as I liked Basel, the Swiss, and my trusted friends, I knew my place was home, in New York, and an internship and residency in New York. It was a huge leap of faith, but I wanted to continue my professional career in New York.

The time was short, I completed the State Board exams in June, finished up my doctor's thesis on familial Thalassemia, and had to start my internship on July 1. My good-byes were short and difficult, especially leaving Nicci, as we were still unmarried (I would return in October to get married). I was finally to begin the next stage of my life in Brooklyn at Maimonides Hospital in the Bay Ridge section of that huge borough.

In July 1962 I returned to a Brooklyn that was as alien to me as a distant planet. Brooklyn was so full of immigrants from all over the world: Jews (Reform and Orthodox), American Blacks, many West Indians, entire neighborhoods of Italians, and even a Norwegian Section! What a culture shock! What a stew of people!! The first thing I heard getting off the subway in the Bay Ridge section of Brooklyn was an Italian woman leaning out of her apartment window yelling, "Ant'ny! Get the hell home before I beat you in your fuckin' head!"

I had accepted a rotating internship at the Maimonides Hospital in Brooklyn, which was difficult, strenuous, and ill paid. We worked every other night at a contracted salary of $3,000 a year. Imagine that! The hospital was remote, in the bay ridge section of Brooklyn; however, Maimonides Hospital Pediatrics did have a Pediatrics professor, Benjamin Kramer, who was a world-renowned expert in Nephrotic syndrome.

I have many stories about the internship and one day will write more about that time, but the first night on call is worth mentioning. Joel Karp and I had graduated from Basel Medical School and accepted the same rotating residency at Maimonides. We were both on call the second night after arrival; neither of us had any practical experience in anything, and we were on surgery that month. We were in the on-call room, which then slept six guys, and the nurse from the ICU called for me to put in an "IV cutdown." I woke Joel and asked, "What is a cut down?" He shook his head, and I told the nurse that I wasn't sure what that was. She must have overheard us talking and told us both to come to the ICU. The seasoned Norwegian nurse told us to watch. She skillfully put in the IV cutdown and saved our asses. And she made sure we knew how to do it before we left. My respect for nurses was never higher. We learned many more practical things in the next weeks. Joel went on to become a famous urologist, and he married the prettiest nurse in the hospital.

In October Nicci called and said she was pregnant. I was elated, confused, scared, happy—all of the above. Certainly, I was also shocked, confused and concerned about Nicci being pregnant again. I decided that I wouldn't allow this to go sour again. I was a doctor of medicine, ready for my career. I agreed immediately that we would marry, told my mother and family, and made preparations to leave for marriage in Locarno. I received permission from my chief of surgery at Maimonides and returned to Switzerland and married Nicci in Orselina, a small village above Locarno in the Italian canton of Tessin.

Now all this occurred in 1962, and America was quite a different country. Years later in 1967, there was an iconic film, *Guess Who's Coming to Dinner*, with Sidney Poitier, Katherine Hepburn, and Spencer Tracy about a black doctor marrying a white girl in the United States when, in twenty-three states, such unions were illegal. I feel that the von Kanitz family was astonished at the events.

My mother and her friend Mrs. Louise Handy met us at Kennedy Airport when we returned home. Mrs. Handy drove through Harlem, an out-of-the-way route to mother's house on Fish Avenue. I didn't understand the reason for driving to Harlem. I can imagine that Maude and Louise wanted to show Nicci where Black people lived, or at least how they lived, and somehow compare it to where we lived in the Bronx. I thought both ideas ludicrous. The term *culture shock* was not in her vocabulary. I remember asking Maude why she had chosen to drive through Harlem, but got only a stone face as a response. I would never know her reasons.

When we arrived at Mother Maude's home, we were met by the scrim of coal dust that frequently drifted over the neighborhood. Though we didn't discuss it, I often wondered what Nicci thought about her first day in the United States. I think it became a lasting impression—she never liked life in the States. The Bronx was—and is still—the epitome of lower middle-class life. Maude wanted to make a statement as to what Nicci was getting herself into. I found it unnecessary and disquieting for a young bride coming from her background. I found it tactless. It was certainly not the image that I thought would make Nicci happy.

I rented a one-bedroom apartment on Remsen Street in Brooklyn Heights. We bought a lovely large sofa from Design Research on Fifty-Seventh Street and Swedish furniture to match. Nicci had her family's chairs from Sweden sent over, which looked great. One year later, while I was a second-year resident at Montefiore Hospital, we moved to a lovely two-bedroom apartment on Pierrepont Street, with a wonderful view of the New York skyline and harbor.

I became a father on March 9, 1963. Christina Natasha Nichols was a normal, spontaneous delivery. She was gorgeous, fat, and round.

Her hair was reddish brown. It became emotional connect-the-dots time. Now that I was a father, I had many thoughts about my own father, wondering where he was and wanting him to know he was a grandfather. I had no ideas or role models for being a father. This was all new territory, a work in progress. I only wished for Nicci and Christina to be strong in the process.

I had no thoughts of finding my father at the time, though. I was making my own history. He had supplied very little to my past and nothing to my present. I was the primogenitor. I was so pleased to be a father. I had great hopes and desires for my child. I was so pleased that all was well.

All in all I was then quite content with life. We met some wonderful friends: Chic and Monika Humboldt, and Fred Sater. Chic was then an acquisitions lawyer for the Bristol-Myers Company. CEO Dick Gelb had bought Clairol for the company and is now himself the CEO of Bristol-Myers Squibb. Fred Sater worked for J P Morgan. We were young lions ready for success.

There were problems, though. I was a struggling resident, and Nicci, who was used to a life of affluence, could never get over what to her was a terrible lack of money. And she did not like New York. I would discover there was no way she could be happy in a relationship—let alone a marriage—with economic restrictions. Nicci did not want to socialize with our new friends or with anyone else. I had a few friends in the neighborhood, mostly illustrators and photographers. One, Lee Baker Johnson, stands out. My friends from the hospital were there too, Rene Gelber and Bill Mesibov. I found them and also kept my old friends that I grew up with. Gilly Anderson had also married a cute, perky Swedish girl, Anita. But Nicci found no liaison, no common ground, with any of them. She kept to herself. She wrote letters to her mother. If we were going to make a marriage, this was the time, but she focused only on her daughter Christina Natasha. We did go to the parks and gardens when I was home and had the time, but Nicci never tried to make a home in New York. In fact, she went home to Bodanas one summer, leaving me alone. She did not like living in Brooklyn Heights.

I clutched and hugged my new baby Christina Natasha after she was born on March 9, 1963. Then I lived through the tragedy of the assassination of our beloved president John Fitzgerald Kennedy on November 22, 1963, and the dramatic funeral with John John saluting. Those were moments for which everyone alive remembers where they were and what they were doing.

Another memorable moment of that time was the blackout on November 9, 1965, when the lights slowly went out over the entire Northeast. I was reading a book on my couch in the apartment on Pierrepont Street and noticed the television rolling the screen. Then I looked out the window and saw the lights on the skyscrapers in lower Manhattan slowly going out street by street. This moment in history was duly documented in the book *The Night the Lights Went Out* by the staff of the *New York Times*. Thirty million people had just as many stories to tell, but there are too many to tell here.

From there, I went to Montefiore for my residency and fellowship in Metabolic Research, and then I received the dreadful news of being drafted into the Medical Corps Army Reserves in January 1966. These were indeed tumultuous times in the lives of most Americans. Lyndon Johnson saw fit to launch a huge array of armed might in Vietnam. He used the Gulf of Tonkin incident to justify the invasion. Most, if not all, of the doctors who were drafted at that time were horrified. We were all against the war in Vietnam and horrified at the disruption of our lives. The alternative options of draft dodging and living in Canada seemed bleak. We grumbled silently and sometimes loudly (though in private), but again this was just one of many rites of passage, like the exams and the rigors of internship and residency, that had to be overcome. Luckily, I was stationed in Germany so I could return to Basel and Switzerland on leave. I saw a lot more of Europe then because I had a Volkswagen Beetle to drive around in.

I remember how devastated I felt upon hearing of the assassination of Robert Kennedy in California. That day I was trying to get an airlift at the huge Torrejón Air Force Base in Spain when the news came over the television. At the airport. I was asked by a bird colonel if I would like a lift to Stuttgart. The deputy NATO Commander, was flying back from Spain after a fishing trip at one of Franco's Estates and wanted to ask me about the tragic events. I was surprised and delighted to fly in a Beech craft Bonanza air jet with four stars on the fuselage. When I was asked up to the front cabin to discuss the assassination with the General, I went into the forward compartment and gave him my opinion based on what I had seen and heard. I thought the situation was dire and the outcome would be bad. He was satisfied with my answer and asked me if there was anything he could do for me. I said I was trying to get to Frankfurt. He said he would see what he could do. I left and went back into the general seating area, with all the brass looking at me—my brief moment of importance.

Getting Drafted, or the Army Experience

I did not feel as much racism in the army as one could expect from the experience in the civilian world. I was a captain in the US Army Medical Corps and was addressed as "Sir." I was always given the deference and respect of my rank. The enlisted saluted the uniform, not the face. I never felt social segregation among the other medical officers, who were in the same situation as the one in which I found myself. We had all been drafted into duty. We were all medical doctors around the same age and at about the same level within the profession. We were all married. And we were obliged to serve.

There was a distance between those of us who had been drafted with the regular army officers and those who were career officers ("lifers"), who were more disciplined and formal in their demeanor and behavior. The men wore shiny shoes and polished brass buttons. The wives wore little hats and gloves and left business cards when visiting. The men always praised their superior officers (who were writing their evaluations), but that is understandable. That was the code. I remember how busy the dispensary was during the day when the dependants of the army personnel in the area would come in as part of their routine, before or after going to the PX to buy things. Military life was as routine as civilian life.

I never thought there was any abject or obvious racism in the army. I did notice that there were very few black officers in the army in general. There were no other black medical doctors in either the Twenty-Fourth General Dispensary or the Ninety-Seventh General Hospital. In the officers' clubs there was never a feeling of racism or ostracism. I did run into young white officers, recently graduated from ROTC programs, who apparently had never had an intelligent conversation with a black doctor (or any black person, for that matter). They were shocked to hear me talk about normal things; this was of course due to their obvious lack of exposure to smart, young black men. I found that even in Switzerland, so I cannot think it was too different. It would be interesting to look at my evaluations from superior officers, which would show how they felt, though it might not offer too much of a boost to my feelings.

There were good times, however. My travels during that time took me many places; a nice trip to London, England, and then to Cambridge in 1967 was a case in point. Nicci and I wanted to see London together. I had been there earlier to see the World Cup soccer final between England and Germany. This time we went there together, seeing the great sights: Hyde Park, Buckingham Palace, the Houses of Parliament, Westminster Abbey, Trafalgar Square, Piccadilly Circus, and Carnaby Street, to name just a few places. I took a lot of slides of the girls in miniskirts and the neighboring pubs. We visited with Fred and Eva Sater, whom we knew from New York. He was now a vice president with J. P. Morgan, and they lived in the fashionable part of town near Kings Road. We visited and shopped and went to the Tate Gallery in the British Museum and saw the Elgin marbles. We went to see *Hair* and danced on the stage at the finale. We visited the Goins, friends from New York who were in the air force, stationed near Cambridge. We visited the university on a typical rainy day, watching the Cambridge boys' choir parade into their dining halls in their high-top hats and tails. We watched the punting on the River Cam, which was quite an experience.

Somewhere in this idyllic period of travel, the real troubles of the world were rearing their ugly heads. There was the great dilemma regarding why the Americans were in fact in Southeast Asia, particularly in Vietnam and Cambodia. There was much civil unrest in the states as Rev. Dr. Martin Luther King Jr. struggled for economic freedom in the south and then was assassinated in Memphis, Tennessee, by someone called James Earl Ray.

In the US Army, we got the news filtered down through the many echelons and in the *Stars and Stripes*. I might've missed some or most of the previous news, but we were indeed aware of the horrors that followed. There were riots in every major city in the United States, and the National Guard was called out in several cities. Fires and killings raged. Thank God I was not home.

In 1968 I took a short vacation in Spain by flying to Madrid and then driving to Seville and back through the mountains and barren countryside. The flights were courtesy of the United States Air Force. I flew on standby from Torrejón, a massive air force base in Madrid, to Stuttgart and then to Frankfurt. I took tours in Toledo with the most beautiful guide I'd ever had. The trip to Seville was a dream, and Seville was so grandiose in its design and magnificent with its Arabic architecture. I took a short trip to Jerez de la Frontera to taste the famous port. The territory between Seville in Madrid is a series of rolling, treeless, arid hills amidst huge, snow-covered mountains—very boring to drive through. Naturally I went to the Corrida de toros and took entirely too many pictures of the bullfight. I arrived at the Terrajon airbase on the day that Robert Kennedy was assassinated by Sirhan Sirhan. I was fortunate to be a doctor that day because I was picked out to be in the party of the deputy chief of NATO, who was returning from a fishing trip at the summer state of Generalissimo Francisco Franco. His colonel thought he might want a medical opinion about the chances of Kennedy recovering from the head shot. I waited with the others aboard a T-39 jet and was called to speak to the four-star general in his forward compartment. He asked me if there seemed to be any chance of survival, and I told him what I thought—from what I had seen on TV, there wasn't a chance that Robert Kennedy could survive the shot. The general looked like Steve Canyon in the comics. He thanked me and asked me if there was anything he could do for me. I asked if he could arrange for some ground transportation and accommodations at his air force base in Stuttgart. "I would be obliged," I said. Sure enough, when I arrived, there was a limo waiting for me. When a full-bird colonel tried to hustle me out of the car, I reminded him and others that the general had ordered it for me. I did, however, graciously invite the colonel to come with me. He accepted.

The most important trip I took, however, was to California. At some point during this time I went on TDY temporary duty to San Francisco to take the California State medical boards. Mark Twain wrote in "Roughing It,":

> The climate of San Francisco is mild and singularly equitable with the thermometer stands at about seventy degrees the year round, it hardly changes at all. You sleep under one or two light blankets summer and winter and never use a mosquito bar [net. Nobody wears summer clothing. You wear black broadcloth if you have it, in August and January, just the same. It is no colder and no warmer in the one-month or in the other. It is as pleasant a climate as well be described in so many places. Take it all around and it is doubtless the most

unvarying in the whole world during eight months of the year straight along the skies are bright and cloudless and never drop of rain falls when the four months come along you will need to go out and steal an umbrella because you will require it not just one day but 120 days in hardly varying succession.

During that visit to San Francisco—I think it was 1967 or '68—I took time off with Steve Silberstein and his wife, Allegra, to visit the center of counterculture, the Haight-Ashbury district of San Francisco. For some it was like Camelot. Upper-middle-class white kids had gathered there in search of a new life: unrestrained sex, lots of drugs like LSD and marijuana, antiwar and anti materialistic sentiments. Utopia to many. The old Victorian houses on the hills, decorated with LOVE signs, became crash pads to celebrate this Summer of Love. We walked around Golden Gate Park and watched a couple get married, serving Maneshevitz grape juice instead of wine. It was so nice to see such young, beaming, happy faces frolicking. They did have flowers in their hair, as Ed Buryn described in his book *Vagabonding in America*, which became a kind of Michelin guide for itinerant young people who took to the road in 1967. He later said, "Most of the people I know have gone on to straight jobs, straight and yuppie." The hippie scene in Haight-Ashbury contrasted with the people and events in Ghirardelli Square, which was undergoing extensive renovations. There were people, mainly Asians, sunning themselves and bravely dancing in the cold surf of San Francisco Bay. Blacks and Latinos played conga drums along the walk as scores of people watched them from the grass. Fisherman's wharf was lively, with lots of tourists and entertainers. The city had a very diverse population of residents who respected each other's lifestyles.

Riding the iconic cable cars up the hills to Russian Hill with its tall glass-front apartment houses was a tonic. Civilization still existed, even in California. I walked all over San Francisco while I was billeted in the BOQ (Bachelor Officers' Quarters) at the Presidio. On one such walk, I saw a crowd in front of a bar and went in to see what was going on. I was astounded by the sight of a new group called the Ike and Tina Turner Revue. I was fascinated by how great the group was. I was sure they would have a great career.

I took the written exam at Del Webb's townhouse in cahoots with a black internist from Los Angeles who drove a new yellow Corvette and was kind enough to take me on a tour of the lovely, fog-shrouded hills of Sausalito. Anyone would love to live or even just visit there. On the way back home I flew to Las Vegas on the military plane. I took pictures at the casinos: the Sands, featuring Danny Kaye, and the new Caesar's Palace on Las Vegas Boulevard. Most of the buildings on the strip were souvenir shops and liquor stores and were not more than two stories high. The Strip sure has changed in the past thirty years; two blocks north or south of the strip used to be desert.

I had been considering moving out to California and starting a practice there; however, when I came out again after my discharge from the army. I was dissuaded by the counterculture that I saw in Los Angeles and San Francisco. But that is another story.

All things good and bad come to an end, so I went back to New York with lots of hope and no tangible prospects.

Nicci and Natasha

During my time in the army and in Germany, I felt that Nicci and I were drifting away from each other. She did not want to be in the army. She did not want to socialize with the other officers' wives. She did not want to live among them. Instead we lived "on the economy" as the expression for living among the Germans and "not on post" goes. We lived in an apartment close to the dispensary and in a penthouse in Bad Homburg. I had twenty-minute commute to the hospital. She stayed at home and read fashion magazines and German society columns in *Elle* (where her cousin Rixa, who was a baroness, worked) and talked with her cousin, Rixa's sister, who lived nearby with her American husband. She went to Sweden a few times when we were there, and I was left alone to eat in the hospital. I got a call from our brother-in-law, Sergio Salvioni, who said that Nicci was going to have an abortion and needed my permission. What could I say but yes, if that was her desire? This was a major event. She seemed to be clearly heading for divorce. When I was "short," that is, just a short time away from being discharged from military duty, Nicci made it clear that she did not want to go back to the United States. I told her that I wanted to start a practice soon in New York, and she asked, "Why don't we go back to Switzerland where I could work in a hospital and live there normally?" I could not agree. She finally said, "I will go back to Bodanas with Natasha" and added that she would take those things that were given to us by her parents and relatives. It was apparent we were breaking up.

After eight years of marriage, Nicci chose not to return with me to the States. She didn't want to live among Americans again, and she refused to leave. Natasha was now eight years old, and as traumatic as it was for her mother and me, it was terrible for a little girl who now believed her father had abandoned her when he went back to the States. Natasha bore the brunt of the marriage breakup, and the scars never seemed to heal. To this day, Natasha is unable to forgive me, and our relationship is almost nonexistent. She lives in Sweden with her boyfriend, Bjorn. They never married and have no children. In fact, of late, I hear that she has left Bjorn and lives alone in Jönköping.

I didn't really think too much about the question of staying on in Switzerland. I wanted to go back to the United States where I thought I belonged. The only question in my mind was whether to practice in New York or California. I had been back to the United States to take my state boards in California, but I had found the state to be a strange place—full of hippies and the free lifestyles of wife swapping and free love. I liked the conservative East Coast.

When I got back to the States, the question before me was whether or not to get a divorce. I got a visit from Nicci's beautiful, tall cousin Baroness Rixa von Treuenfels, who visited me on Central Park West. She suggested that Nicci and I try to get together again and work things out. I said I would try again, although I didn't think things could be worked out. Even when we had been living in the States, during summer vacations in Southampton or Long Island, or on trips to Sardinia and Mallorca, Nicci met my efforts not with rapprochement, but with sullen pouting and indifference. I did, however, fly to Zermatt, where I stayed in the same hotel with her and Natasha. We skied and drank with old friends (the Hans and Greta Chi-tsun family) and visited with Nicci's family member, Princess Reuss, who was vacationing there for the season. But what I had once thought was Nicci's Greta Garbo sophistication was really a self-absorbed shallowness. Nicci did not want a reconciliation, and no attempts of mine to keep us together as a married couple and as parents ever seemed to work. It was then that I finally realized the situation was futile and that she and I did not share the same vision. Her concept of being a doctor's wife had nothing to do with the reality of the years of struggle and hard work. She refused to grow with me. Still, I had no intention of divorcing at that time—the truth was that for me, even though Nicci and I were separating, I still fantasized about having a family—one with a history, a place in Sweden to go home to, a refuge from the problems of the work in the States—at least a family that had roots. It was becoming clear to me that this was a fantasy and that my quest for myself and my roots would be in America. I had no real roots except educational and cultural roots and even social roots in Europe. My home was in the US.

Chapter Eight

GAYLE

I met Jeannine Gayle Porter, who worked in the obstetric delivery room of the Ninety-Seventh General Hospital, at this time. She was a civilian nurse. She looked so cute in her Ob "blues" that I had to take her picture. She was beautiful and had a gorgeous figure. We flirted with each other, exchanging witticisms and jokes, and it soon became apparent that we were both looking for company. We were both in the midst of breaking up existing relationships. We had drinks together in the officers' club and joked with her ex-boyfriend, Ron Cox, who was also a draftee internist at the hospital.

A diary entry from this time reads:

> Gayle charmed me to death with her West Virginia accent. Spoke of her home and her family as if it was straight out of *Little House on the Prairie*. I met her often in the Officers Club and soon we were seeing each other often. I had to stay in the hospital area while I was on duty so I took my call in the BOQ and her BOQ room. Our relationship grew.

She was very shy. She later explained that she was not used to socializing or having friends since she came from a very small town in "West by God Virginia" with the unlikely name of Salt Rock. She was very homespun and plain in her dress, which was part of her charm. She was quite a contrast to anyone I had ever known. Gayle's freshness brought a sense of hope for a new beginning.

My relationship with Gayle continued to grow in wonderful and happy ways. I had been in New York for several months when I got a letter that she wanted to stop by New York on her way back to North Carolina, where she had trained. I showed her my world in New York, which she loved. Her stop transformed into a stay which was amazing to me. I was somehow mesmerized. Part of her West Virginia charm.

She moved into my apartment on the West Side and shopped with me for Persian rugs and furniture in all the smart shops in Manhattan. We bought two Siamese cats and named them Sagamore (because his ears made me think of him as an Indian chief with a headdress) and Split (her quirk of darting away from all danger perceived or imagined..). We filled the apartment with large plants and a tropical fish tank. We loved the local restaurants and being able to walk over to Central Park in the spring, summer, and fall and watch the flower children, and listen to the black and Latino musicians who played around the fountain. I built a large model sailing boat and sailed it on the children's pond in the park. These were the halcyon days for me. I believe they were for Gayle too. We lived well, ate well—and I drank too much, a legacy of being in and having access to liquor at ridiculously cheap PX prices. (I also had a genetic predisposition to alcoholism, which I found out about when I traced my father in 1994 and '95.)

As my relationship with Gayle grew, my feelings for Nicci waned. I had mixed emotions, though and felt caught in an emotional tug of war— torn between not wanting to divorce, yet knowing that Nicci and I were forever separated, and that I was now estranged from my only child, a little girl who would one day certainly feel I abandoned her.

It makes sense at this point to share my thoughts about marriage, as pertains to women in general and the two that I married. Marriage comes with expectations from both parties—and then there is the reality. I don't think that Nicci ever thought too clearly about what life with me in America would be like for her, pregnant and without a job. I don't think she had any concept about starting a new life with any man, white or black, in the United States. Her orientation was clear: she was a European who had grown up in a genteel society of nobility. She had no concept of having little money. Her idea of being a doctor's wife was that it came with instant wealth and the good life. She had no idea that a young doctor has years of training to endure before he starts paying for his loans. She could not bear the strain it imposed on her to have little or no money. I made $3,000 a year when I started out as an intern, and each year after that got an additional thousand dollars a year. In the army I made $10,000 as a captain in the United States Army Medical Corps, but the shock of being in the army with strange people not of her ilk was repulsive to Nicci. And the thought of coming back to the same problems when I was discharged was too much to endure. It would a strain she was not prepared to bear. I suppose she could have lived on her mother's estate until I was earning more money and could afford a better life, but reality and events caught up with her. The reality was that I was not going to be left alone for any stretch of time waiting for Godot. My expectations were different.

Gayle, on the other hand, was so willing to endure residency and beginning life as the girlfriend and eventual wife of a young doctor while she worked as a nurse. Her expectations were that she would have a baby and then settle down with the child in a new home in the suburbs, buy a station wagon, and be happy. Here the key word is *expectations*.

In 1972 Gayle and I flew down to Montego Bay in Jamaica and spent a wonderful week in the broiling hot Jamaican sun. We visited Dr. John and Mrs. Louise Moseley, who had a vacation home there. John took us to his favorite places. We swam in the beautiful waters, drove to the capital, Kingston, and had lovely dinners in the famous tropical Blue Mountains (where, arguably, the finest and most expensive coffee in the world comes from). We took another trip to Quebec, by car, and visited the castle of a young woman I had met on a flight to Europe. The beautiful castle was on the shore of the St. Lawrence River. Quebec itself was the closest thing to Europe in the Americas.

A diary entry from this time reads:

> One would think that all we did was travel during those wonderful years, and in large measure one would be right. Indeed we did have a lot more money and no children, so of course we took advantage of it. Most of the time we lived in New York City on Central Park West, working in our respective jobs at the Neighborhood Health Services Program—a new concept of community medicine which was designed to deliver good health care to the under served neighborhoods and was backed by a local large University affiliated teaching hospital—and at the New York Health Department. On weekends we'd leave the city and spend a lot of time at the home of some of my old friends who lived in New Rochelle, where we eventually hoped to own a home ourselves and settled down.

When I was told that a nice place was for sale in New Rochelle, we went to see it and were overjoyed at how wonderful it was. There were beautiful flowers blooming in the garden; the living room walls were paneled, and the place had four bedrooms. We were overjoyed. After looking at my finances and savings I applied for and got a mortgage.

We moved to New Rochelle after two hours of nerve-wracking, finger-shaking signing of the different ownership and financing papers. After getting good advice from my real estate lawyers, I got title insurance too.

But it was Gayle I was enamored of, growing closer to her all the time. Our marriage was inevitable. She anchored me in the soil of America. I mean that in the true sense. When I bought the house in New Rochelle, I went back to gardening. working with my hands, painting and paneling the attic and the cellar, and so on. She was there at my side, often showing me how to repair something, as her father had taught her. This was her preordained role in our marriage. She was a Mrs. Fix-It.

> *I shall be telling this with a sigh*
> *Somewhere ages and ages hence:*
> *Two roads diverged in the woods, and I—*
> *I took the one less traveled by,*
> *And that has made all the difference.*

> —Robert Frost, "The Road Not Taken" (1916)

Gayle: Her Life, Our Marriage, and Her Death

My relationship with Gayle grew over the ensuing years in New York. There were other wonderful trips during those years: Rio de Janeiro in Brazil, California, Barbados. Gayle and I were married in 1974 at the Riverside Church.

In 1976, when I looked back on the previous year, I was moved to write in my diary, "Last year was filled with discord, crime, terrorism, inflation and declining world enthusiasm, but still, all in all, we are doing well. The brightest spot was the birth of Christiana Celeste in 1975."

Remembrances of a married past.

Gayle and I were married at the Riverside Church on June 9, 1974, and settled into raising our family. Christy was born in 1975 and Meredith in 1978. We had a comfortable home in New Rochelle, with lots of room for gardening, which Gayle and I loved to do, and space for swings, surface swimming pools, and games. It was not all fun and games, though. Gayle was incredible in the house and garden. There wasn't anything that she had not done or fixed with her father in Salt Rock, West Virginia. We planted the garden and paneled the attic and the cellar walls. I even built recycled drawers for clothes, and cabinets for the TV as well as the hi-fi and amplifier. We lived through three recessions and lots of struggles with the practice and her working in the hospital. The practice of medicine changed dramatically. We had to contend with the change to the more corporate view of practice. The powers that be decided to allow health maintenance organizations (HMOs) to link with the various insurance companies and create panels of specialists that would serve as health care providers for patient care. The transition was difficult and at first was resisted, but sooner or later all physicians in private practice and in the hospitals succumbed. I might add that I joined most HMOs and did fairly well in these years as the practices grew.

Nonetheless, life was not what we planned. We spent most of our leisure time reading books. She enjoyed science fiction, and I preferred to read about history as warfare, and enjoyed fantasy and adventure books too. When we were in the house, this was our mental hideaway, our hidey-hole from our many fears and anxieties. Gayle was always paranoid about some disaster occurring. She joked about it when she was not chewing her fingernails. She had seen a psychiatrist while in nursing school at Duke. She always said, "It is not paranoia when they are really chasing you." For my part, I had episodes of urticaria and heartburn; only later did I start taking Zantac and other antacids. Nonetheless, the girls never suffered too much, though they were aware of the financial problems we always seemed to have. They saw us gnashing our teeth and grumbling not so silently over bills.

We shared our fun times with other couples we knew: the Toyloys, Sam and Nancy MacFadden, Bill and Elie Smith, who had been in school with my brother and me in Switzerland, Joe and Jean Hurd in Massachusetts, Bill and Arlette Brown in Queens, Glen and Juanita Hale, and Patsy and Buster Richardson. We all had small children, and we were all doctors and businessmen starting their professional careers. We took summer vacations, mostly to Disney World and later to Mazatlan and Cancun in Mexico, Martha's Vineyard and the Carolinas, the Canary Islands, Oahu, Hawaii. Many times we went with another couple, the Lorieos, with their two boys, and we have bonded as a family ever since. There were nice times with the group, and we managed to see each other often for barbecues, holiday dinners, and vacations. We enjoyed the 1980s. These were the halcyon years. We raised several litters of Siamese cats from Sagamore and Split. And later from Beast and Beauty. I bought Beast in 1983 when Meredith was in kindergarten. Gayle was working the night shift at Montefiore. I brought a seal point kitten to replace Sagamore, who had died of renal failure at the vet's. The girls were so distressed and upset that I had to buy a replacement. Beast loved the girls. We later bought a second mate for Beast and named her Beauty. It was great having them around the house. They were great hunters of mice and other small critters in the backyard and vied with many other neighborhood cats that roamed around.

One August, I took Gayle and the girls for a brief trip to South Carolina in hopes of long walks on pretty beaches. Instead it rained every day. We were at a miserable coastal resort in Myrtle Beach, and we spent hours looking at nothing but dark, dismal clouds that stretched endlessly down the beach. The high point of the trip was our visit to Brookgreen Gardens, a two-hundred-year-old rice plantation that had been beautifully, and lovingly restored to its earlier splendor. Moss-draped oak trees, magnolias, azaleas, and camellias echoed the plantation's former glory. I could imagine all the poor slaves who had drained the swamp, planted the rice, and toiled endlessly to create such a lovely place. The gardens hold the largest permanent outdoor collection of American figurative sculpture. We took long walks through the acres and acres of lush gardens. It almost made up for the first few days of wretched weather.

In the nineties we managed somehow throughout the successive recessions in the economy. It was quite a feat to get the girls through high school and send them to Cornell and Tufts. They then went to medical school and physical therapy school and became doctors, so we could not complain too much. Gayle never lived long enough to see the fruition of her long struggle. She had endured a twenty-year-long struggle with asthma, and then because of her long treatment with steroids, developed aseptic necrosis in her right hip. She had a hip replacement and suffered some hearing loss after surgery and prolonged anesthesia. It seemed that she had either experienced an anoxic episode or a few mini strokes. Her mental condition never fully recovered thereafter, and she began suffering memory loss and slowness of cognition. We all thought it normal for her, as she was getting older—she was in her fifties—but her condition deteriorated slowly but inexorably.

It had been a long time coming. Gayle did not like "being in this body anymore." She often did not know who she was or where she was. This was an extremely difficult time, and for years we had no idea what was going on. Gayle had developed soft signs of some mental disorder years before we were told of the diagnosis. In the ten years before her death in 2005 the kids and I were aware that she was different and becoming more forgetful, desperately trying to remember things by writing them down. She had several notebooks in which she wrote down things she wanted to remember, but would lose them too. She would sometimes burn the dinners she prepared, though she had always taken pride in her "down home" cooking. Her usual sharp thinking was changing, but we thought it was just her getting older and sort of slowing down. We had no idea that it was part of the disease process. Gayle had been so sharp in her mental ability, with a sharp mind that absorbed so much. She read all the science fiction books she could get her hands on—printed in paperback, in *Reader's Digest*, anything. She was always reading. In social conversation she was usually well equipped to sit silently until she let out an incredibly incisive remark that cut to the quick. No one underestimated her intelligence.

And that stopped! She shut down—a description I never fully understood until then. We were indeed shocked when in February things took a turn for the worse. We had a two-week time-share in Barbados, and I was hoping to go there and continue work on my memoir, which at the time was still untitled. She didn't like going to Barbados and certainly did not like being in the sun ever. She lived in constant fear of melanoma since she had gotten a basaliom excised some years before.

We agreed that I should go and she would be okay. I got a call at the time-share resort in the second week that she had been found walking alone in the neighborhood by one of the neighborhood boys from across the street. She was disoriented. Christy, who also got the message, and my brother responded and called me. I came home two days later and found a totally different Gayle.

After a rather dramatic turn, she was hospitalized and diagnosed with dementia and Alzheimer's disease. We were flabbergasted at the term *dementia* being offered by the psychiatrist. It was only later that her neurologist put everything together and diagnosed Lewy body disease, which is a combination of Alzheimer's and Parkinson's disease. Her condition and medical course nose-dived rapidly, and within a year she hardly recognized us. We had hired a home attendant, Diane Wrencher, who cared for Gayle tirelessly, 24/7. She has lived with us since then. After four years of increasing difficulty, Gayle suddenly collapsed at home and died. Her struggle was over. It was a very sad moment for Christy, Meredith, and me to endure. We bonded even closer in those times and ever since. We interred her ashes near a Chinese maple tree we bought in St. John's Episcopal on North Avenue, where we worshiped when the need was felt.

Chapter Nine

STARTING PRACTICE

I suffered from culture shock when I returned from Germany after serving three years in the US Army Medical Corps at Frankfurt General Hospital. I had separated from Nicci, who decided that she would go back to Sweden to live with her mother in Bodanas. She just could not hack being back in New York. It was her decision. Life goes on.

Manhattan was not the Bronx or even Brooklyn. The West Side of Manhattan is a world to itself. Frankly, I prefer the Upper West Side, with its intellectual, artistic, humanistic, and poetic character.

I had decided that I wouldn't go back to my fellowship in metabolic research at Montefiore, which I am sure discomfited my mentor Larry Finberg, but I had to make more money that I had when I was a fellow. The cab driver from the airport told me he made $30,000 a year, and my fellowship paid only $15,000. I was sorry to have to leave the brilliant Dr. Finberg, but I felt I could not go into academic medicine (it had not even kept me out of the army).

Of course there were other reasons why I wanted to go into clinical medicine and see patients. I had no interest in working in a hospital. I did not like hospital politics, with the staff and administrative squabbles and the meetings and ad hoc committees. I have an old report card from 3B indicating that my ability to work well with others "needs improvement."

I guess I was a libertarian like Ayn Rand. The other main reason was that my army experience working in the Twenty-Fourth General Dispensary and later at the Ninety-Seventh General Hospital in Frankfurt had given me the opportunity to work in a clinic seeing patients, dependents of US Army personnel—people from all over the United States and indeed anywhere the army had been deployed—an interesting sample of humanity. I found my vocation and that was to one day practice pediatrics in my own office in New York.

So on the advice of Harry Delaney, who became an attending surgeon while I was in the army, recommended that I speak to Doris Weathers at St. Luke's Hospital because there were openings for clinical pediatricians in the local satellite clinics. In turn, Doris Weathers, who had done extensive work in sickle-cell anemia, recommended that I speak to Gil Fuld, who was a director at the Neighborhood Health Services Program at 160 West 100th Street. I did and started to work there after two weeks, with a salary of $25,000. The clinic serviced the Hispanic population in the neighborhood, mostly Puerto Ricans but a few Dominicans and South Americans as well. I learned about salsa and pernil and began to learn broken Spanglish. I rented an apartment at 400 Central Park West, learned more about Central Park, and listened to the wonderful summer concerts. I also discovered the action on the West Side. Lots of cool, well-educated black and white people lived in the neighborhood. I saw a lot of the old gang I knew, who had moved nearby. I went to the jazz places—Under the Stairs, the Cellar, and Mikell's—and slowly got used to being a civilian and separated from my wife and child, who had stayed in Sweden. The culture shock I experienced upon returning to New York lasted for months, if not a full year. And I still dressed in army green: I bought green shirts and pants from Sears, and the nurses at the hospital thought I was a maintenance man.

While I was working in the Neighborhood Services Program on 100th Street, I received a call from the chief of pediatrics at St. Luke's Hospital, Dr. Stuart Symington.

He said, "Dr. Nichols, could you see a private patient for me? I have a lady on the line who would like her son to be seen by a black pediatrician, and I thought that perhaps you could see her son. Would you be interested?"

I replied, "Sure, why not—but where?"

He said, "You could see her in the private doctor's offices in 1090, Amsterdam Avenue, across the street from the hospital. I will arrange for her to me you on the fourth floor. Her name is Mrs. Cauldwell, and her son's name is Paul Cauldwell."

I was so happy and excited to see my first private patient.

I met the elegant Mrs. Cauldwell at the appointed time and saw her son, who had experienced a mild to moderate acute asthma attack. I gave him the treatment that was appropriate for that time and age, and he was relieved of his symptoms. I wrote a prescription on the office's prescription pad and wanted to wish them well, when Mrs. Cauldwell asked me, "Well, how much do I owe you?"

I had never in my life received payment for treatment from a patient, so I said, "I don't know."

Mrs. Cauldwell said, "Well, I usually pay twenty dollars," which she promptly put in my hand. She then said, "When should I come back for a recheck?"

Now I became really flustered. I had no idea as to where and how I could see this patient. However, Mrs. Cauldwell seemed so assured that I said, "I will check with Dr. Stuart, and perhaps I can see you next week."

Well, I did see them again, and she told me that she would tell all of her friends that she had met a nice, young black doctor at St. Luke's Hospital and they would certainly like their children to be seen. It helped that her husband was the pastor at Grace Baptist Church on 138th Street. She was certainly good on her word, and soon I was quite busy on the West Side of New York City.

I then started a pediatric practice in 1970 in the doctor's offices at 1090 Amsterdam Hospital across from St. Luke's Hospital, and later I moved to a huge suite on Claremont Avenue. The eight-story building had been built in 1896 by Aiello and had two apartments on each floor. The rooms were large with high ceilings. The walls were wainscoted in oak, which added a lot of elegance. I was so happy to get such a large, luxurious office.

That is how I started seeing patients, and it has not stopped in thirty-one years. I was also given a running start by Gil Fuld, a pediatrician at St. Luke's who was relocating to Keene, New Hampshire. He gave me—at no cost—the charts of some hundreds of his patients from the West Side of Manhattan. He went through his lists of patients and mentioned things about each of them. I was amazed how he could remember all the small details and different aspects about them: what the parents did for a living, what kind of character the child had, and so on. It was only after I had been in practice for a few years that it dawned on me how it could be so easy to remember these details—it's because you care about them and wonder about them and their futures.

The practice at Claremont Avenue was part-time and very middle class. Grace Cauldwell's friends spread the word in New York that I had opened a practice in the huge, luxurious office in the historic Columbia University building on Claremont Avenue. I had lots of referrals from Cab Callaway's daughter, Lael Calloway, who was my first medical assistant, and their theatrical and musical friends. Many Columbia University professors brought their children. I did get nice referrals from Woman's Hospital. Things were happening. I took less time at the Neighborhood Services Health Program Clinic and worked in the afternoons and evenings at Claremont. My future seemed secure. But one can never predict the economy, and I became very aware of economic changes in the world. The words *inflation* and *recession* became very biting, horrible reminders to me.

When things were good, people came to the office and paid in cash or good checks. In bad times I was soon to learn that they either didn't come or didn't pay. In fact I found out later that doctors were the last to be paid when things were tough. "After all," people said, "he's a doctor and has plenty of money." No one thought that doctors had bills to pay, even in bad times.

After Lael left for her singing career, I had a string of part-time students that helped me run the front office. I saw patients, and on Saturdays and some evenings, was joined by Terry Wilson, a registered nurse I had met at St. Luke's Hospital. We were all amateurs.

It was easy to keep one person in charge because the girls would have to leave and take other courses or graduate and move on. As luck would have it, one of the nicer parents recommended her sister-in-law, Erika Martin, who was looking for a new job.

Erika transformed the practice from a philanthropic enterprise to a business. I had no idea what that meant. I thought I had a profession and a practice and that money would somehow come to me. I realized that I was naive as to pricing schedules, how to get bills paid, and how to get people to pay me. It soon became apparent that I had thousands of dollars outstanding because there was no system of accounts receivable. Erika had previous experience working with other doctors in Manhattan and developed her expertise in the office. She organized the confusion, paid the bills, and collected the outstanding bills. The parents were shocked and pleased by her efficiency. It was a constant learning process; the rules were constantly changing.

She made me realize that I didn't have enough patients at the Claremont office to sustain a livelihood alone. This was so prophetic: three years later another budget squeeze forced me out of the Neighborhood Health Services Program to fend for myself. This was a bitter experience and changed the course of my life. This was indeed one of the many rough patches I had to plod through in my professional life.

I was grateful to have Erika there to help me through this dire period. I never had Medicaid patients at the Claremont office; I saw Medicaid patients at the clinic. There was a transition from my very high middle class practice.

Erika was optimistic and far more patient than I was. She did her best to assuage my doubts and fears. "Dr. Nichols," she would say, "it's summer. People would rather be at the beach or at a pool than sitting in a doctor's office."

For sixteen years Erika worked with me, sharing all the pain and frustration. We endured through all the changes in the practice. We went from fee-for-service billing to insurance claims and waded through Medicaid rate changes, the introduction of managed care, and computerization of the office billing system. She was so vital to the practice.

Erika taught me one fundamental thing, and it was this: "It doesn't matter how much make and how long you work—it is a question of lifestyle." She told me that I would never become a millionaire, which didn't surprise me but did hurt my pride for a few hours. She also gave me good advice that I should not work such long hours so that I would not burn out. All of this was sage advice that I apparently needed to hear.

Erika passed away in 1994 after a yearlong struggle with inoperable gallbladder cancer. She has been and will continue to be sorely missed.

I have written about my preference for private practice earlier. I do want to add a few things about this subject. I felt like a stranger working at St. Luke's, I had not trained there and did not know the attending physicians in pediatrics or in the other specialties too well. In fact, in the first year of my association with St. Luke's, I would call my colleagues at Montefiore for any consultations. This was mostly out of familiarity, but I found out that St. Luke's did not have the depth of specialties available for consultation. The level of expertise was not the level I had grown used to. Sadly, over the years, the existing level of expertise sank lower. The department had poor leadership and little financing from the hospital. They could not hire any specialists and gradually lost the accreditation that is so necessary to a level one or two hospital. In fact the hospital itself was going through a financial crises and lost its nursing school and, soon after, the teaching program in pediatrics and ob-gyn. Hospitalists were hired to run the wards. It was a sad culmination. The pediatric department of Roosevelt Hospital was fused together, but that did not help the situation.

Danne Lorieo who Is a general surgeon at St. Lukes Hospital and a lifelong friend of mine and my daughters, shared this:

> When the new hospital was opened in 1992, Pediatrics and OB-Gyn were moved to Roosevelt in spite of the tradition of Woman's hospital at St Luke's. The Harlem community sued St. Luke's-Roosevelt for this diminution of services and eventually Pediatrics was moved back to St Luke's.

The only saving grace was the neonatal department, which grew into a megalith unto itself. But that meant that private pediatricians were shut out of taking care of the newborns. All or most newborns were seen by neonatologists and later the hospitalists, so the connection with the private voluntary doctors became tenuous at best.

Practice of Medicine in Harlem

It's easy to look back on the last four decades of practice in Harlem and the West Side of Manhattan. It was an extravaganza of different people, thoughts, ideas, cultures, languages, and religions.

In 1982, ten years after I began my New York practice, I added an additional office on Strivers' Row in Harlem. I had heard that Dr. Thomas Patrick, who had a pediatric practice on 139th Street, was going to retire. He had been there in practice since 1937! He too had gone to school in Europe. graduating from the University of Berlin in 1936. After a long and protracted negotiation (he really didn't want to retire), we signed a contract whereby I bought his practice, including the old telephone number that everyone in Harlem knew for $25,000, which I paid over three years. I was happy that I was able to continue a tradition. I was also fulfilling a mission and a prediction that was unknown to me at the time. This announcement appeared in the *Harlem Amsterdam News*:

Dr. Edward Atkinson Nichols, a close associate and friend of the Patrick family, will inherit the tradition of more than 45 years of good child health care for Harlem's babies on 139th Street. Not only do both doctors share a sincere desire to bequeath a legacy of good health care to the Harlem community; but they share many other interesting parallels in their life, as well as a father-son relationship. Dr. Nichols is married with two daughters, age seven and four: Christiana and Meredith.

This Was Harlem by Jervis Anderson offers this insight into the iconic neighborhood:

Strivers Row is the name that poorer Harlemites gave to the tree lined blocks of 138th and 139th Streets between Seventh and Eight Avenues. On these blocks were (are) some of the finest houses in Harlem. Designed by Sanford White, among other architects, for the developer David H. King Jr., they had been built in 1891 as homes for Harlem's white well-to-do. In 1918, when the black invasion of Harlem began to send whites fleeing from 138th and 139th Streets, the houses were taken over by the Equitable Life Insurance Company. They even began renting to blacks in 1919, as the Kings Court Houses. Prominent doctors such as Louis T. Wright, Wiley Wilson and the Architect Verner Tandy (he had designed the St. Philips's Protestant Episcopal Chapel) and Madame C. J. Walker's Mansion Villa Lewaro, William Pickens and musicians Noble Sissle. Adam Clayton Powell Jr. wrote in 1945 "Concentrated in Striver's Row … were dowagers of Harlems Society. These queenly, sometimes portly, and nearly always light skinned Czarrinas presided over the Harlem upper Class.

I had searched first in Europe and later in the mountains of West Virginia for a homeland where people loved me and I felt at home, but it was in Harlem that I really found the homeland I had been seeking. This was where my Mother Maude had W. C. Handy's wife, Louise Handy, drive me through 138th Street where she lived when Nicci first came to New York. She was wiser than I in wanting to show me my homeland. Perhaps even more symbolic was that I finally accepted being black in Harlem as my homeland.

The population of the practice represented a microcosm of the black communities in the United States. Their problems, feelings, and attitudes mirrored the socioeconomic problems of most of the black urban centers in America. When I was a young man I read books by E. Franklin Frazier about the talented tenth and others by Dr. Kenneth Clark, professor of sociology at CCNY. I knew about the strata of black folk on paper and had seen it from afar. But here it was up close and personal, like Oliver Cromwell said when they were to paint his picture, "warts and all." Harlem indeed had and has its social strata that live cheek by jowl. There are projects next to private condominiums. Whose bright idea was that? They don't have that on Park Avenue. The hoodlum and the eighteen-year-old girl with three babies by different men at living and walking in the same street with a middle-class lawyer, Mason, civil service clerk, postman, teacher, and the overdressed church lady.

I am no stranger to Harlem.

I do remember when I was a student at CCNY walking down 140th Street from Convent Avenue while I was a teenager, to meet my mother at Jocks at the corner of 138th Street, where we had delicious chicken, peas and rice, and collards. I remember Mother taking me to a dance at the Renaissance across the street at 138th Street when I was a young boy and watching an "exotic dancer" (or was she a stripper?). Imagine that. What a mom! I wonder what she was thinking.

In those teenage years I came down from the Bronx on the D Train to dance at the Ivy Delph Apartments community room with girls from Convent Avenue, Strivers' Row (138th and 139th Streets), the Riverton apartments, and Sugar Hill (555 Edgecombe Avenue). Clothilde Guinnier Stevenson, Jane Moseley, Anita Philyaw, Barbara Boozer Brown, Billy Brooks, Paul Dawson, Roy Woodruff, Sandra Day, Paula Romero, Raymond Romero, Billy Dee Williams, Loretta Williams, Leonard Reilly, Pat Simmons, and Toni Willis Brown—we had a blue light on and thought we were cool, grinding with a willing partner and smoking. Others reminded me there were some class distinctions drawn, sorting by color, black bourgeois, and schooling. Fair skin was in, and brown, out. If you lived on the Hill you were considered special. Past 155th Street you were marginal. It was a time of growing pains for blacks. We were still segregated socially, and as young people of color we wanted to spread our wings and be a part of a bigger world. And let us not forget about *hair*. Straight and curly. We are a group of people obsessed about hair, even today. There were always discussions among the guys Gilly, Billy, Junius, and so on, who were all lighter complexioned than me, about how this or that girl who was of this or that color, or how the pretty girls were usually lighter skinned. Now there was a little confusion in my mind about color because my mother was very light skinned and had passed as white for most of her life. This was a sad problem for me and for the rest of my friends and community, apparently. I never had the problem of color, which was foisted upon me by my peers and society around me.

As if skin color was not enough, there was the question of how "good" your hair was. What kind of question is that? Yet that question is still being asked today, black men going from Afros to the current baldness. I did not like the way the Italian barbers cut my hair in the Bronx and went to a barbershop on Seventh Avenue and 135th Street to have Tolbert cut my hair. I learned about horse racing with the constant calling of the races on the radio. I even read *Jet* magazine (that's where I saw the dreadful pictures of Emmett Till).

I remember the racism of those times. White kids suddenly broke off contact with colored kids when they became teenagers. It seemed sudden when I came across it at parties, when white girls refused to dance with me or turns at spin the bottle froze me out. The professional colored people formed a club with other middle-class kids, so they could get together. We then had little choice but to go to the get-togethers of these disparate groups. Many have written in books such as *Our Kind of People* about the Girlfriends organization and the Jack and Jill bunch.

I hadn't been in Harlem such a long time. Coming back made me so nostalgic. I was reminded of my mother meeting me for dinner in the famous Red Rooster Restaurant when I was at CCNY in the fifties and going with her to her social gatherings at the Renaissance Ballroom on

Seventh Avenue and 138th Street and the Savoy Ballroom on Lenox Avenue and 140th Street, the air redolent with the smells of sweet potatoes, fried fish, pork chops, cornbread, waffles, hominy grits, collard greens, and the sounds of Duke Ellington and Count Basie.

The Cotton Club was built on the Northeast corner of 142nd and Lenox Avenue to compete with the very successful Renaissance Casinos, which was at 138th Street and Seventh Avenue. The Club was owned and operated by Owney Madden, a mobster and a bootlegger from Hell's Kitchen. The Cotton Club was famous for its major attraction, Cab Calloway, with his famous "Minnie the Moocher" routine.

Establishing a new practice or reestablishing an old one is so difficult. Medical school did not prepare me for having a practice. Everything was a learning experience. and maintaining the balance between practice and home was as tough as balancing a checkbook.

The first day of taking over Dr. Patrick's practice filled me with a combination of great expectation and equally great anxiety. I'm afraid things got off to a very slow start, which fed my frustration and had me wondering if I hadn't made a huge mistake. I began thinking that maybe I shouldn't have taken over Dr. Patrick's practice.

The Practice at 139th Street

I had heard from one the regular salesmen, Ted Munro, that there was a practice in Harlem that was coming available. He and I had talked about my expanding somewhere because there were a limited amount of patients that would come to the Claremont office, and the Columbia parents did not show any desire to come to my office. (I wondered whether this was due to racism.) Ted told me about Dr. Patrick, who had been a fixture in Harlem for decades. I did meet with Tom Patrick and his lawyer ; we entered into negotiations, and finally I signed a contract to buy his office for $25,000.

Tom was a venerable, distinguished, tall, handsome, elegant man. He was also a glad hander—that is, a bullshitter—and quite a character, as I learned. Some could say unkindly that he was a charlatan. The people of Harlem loved him. He wrote articles in the *New York Amsterdam News* about caring for children and a program called "Yes You Can" that promoted exercise and health.

Erika Martin Talavera, my constant and loyal medical assistant, and I spruced up the office as best we could on short notice. The walls had been stripped bare of the photographs and posters that Tom had put up. His old files in still older file cabinets were folders with no continuity; pages were just inserted haphazardly. His notes were his shorthand chicken scratches; and when asked about it, he winked and said it was "so people would not know what he thought of them." People loved him and sang his praises. He told some people that I was his son. Nonetheless, the practice was well known, and the telephone number and address would be the same. It was still like starting a brand-new practice from scratch. Harlem however has a—I hesitate to use the phrase—jungle telegraph. Word got out that the new doctor was there at Dr. Patrick's old practice. Gradually, after a long, hot summer, patients began coming in. Oh, happy day.

Starting out in the middle of August is not the best time. Most everyone in the city is either on vacation, visiting relatives in the South, or (if they are kids) in some summer camp. Some children were in school because they had flunked some subject. In any event, they did not intend to spend their time in a pediatrician's office. I looked out the window of the office and moaned, "What have I done? Was this the answer?" Doubts came and filled the room with despair.

I remember, when I had been in the practice for several months and parents would ask Erika, who was born in Venezuela. questions about me: *Is he white? What race is he? Where was he born and raised?* I decided to put up pictures and collages of my ancestors of all hues and mixtures, and I began to go through making the introductions to my patients and their parents. Fortunately, I had made collages of old daguerreotypes, which my mother had given me, of my great-grandfather and great-grandmother and put them together with pictures of my grandfather and grandmother when they were young, along with small pictures of my mother, Aunt Mae, and Uncle Roy. I also had pictures of my mother and father during their lives. It was an interesting collection. All of the pictures reminded me of my grandmother, around whom our family revolved. She was indeed the matriarch of us all.

The children of the neighborhood were so different from the patients at Claremont. I really felt the class difference. What do I mean by that seemingly elitist remark? The children at 139th Street seemed less vocal, less articulate, and less engaging. They had problems communicating. I had developed the habit of asking any child above four or five, "Why did you come here today?" They usually would not respond, but would turn away or look to their parents for the answers. The parents would say, "Tell the doctor why you are here!" They would look down and offer some simple answer like "I don't know" or "What?" I would say, "Well, okay, I'll ask you again. And when they were on the examining table I would do just that. In the meantime the parents usually clued the children in.

Most, if not all, of Dr. Patrick's patients were on Medicaid. Many were behind in their immunizations. Many had not been seen for a long time. There were many who came with housing problems, problems needing letters from doctors for housing, bus passes, elevator passes, and so on. Many of the fathers of these children were absent because they had left the mothers and had other families, or the fathers had been killed or incarcerated on some drug, theft, or homicide charge. Many kids had social, psychiatric, or learning problems. I said "Wow!" many times in the first few years.

This is not to say that being poor makes you dumb—but, let's face it, poverty puts a kid at a big disadvantage. I was never poor by any definition, and I am sure I had many disadvantages as compared to rich kids.

I like talking to little people who like to talk. "I'm a little girl, and I am four and a half, and I like to talk." "Now I want to show how I can …" "Look here, let me tell you …"

I was like a babe in the woods, naive and unaware of so many things. My libertarian ideas of pulling yourself up by your own bootstraps, like I thought I had done, were thrown out the window. I was told that in the summer the next block—140th Street, between Seventh and Eighth Avenue * —would change into Fort Apache at night. Gunfire, cops, raids. Pandemonium. I was hesitant to have hours after dark. Mothers, mostly single parents, would tell me how awful their situations were, how desperate things were. "My husband was killed," they would say, or "He is in prison for life." They felt trapped. "I was so in love, and he left me." Many had three or four children; some were teenage girls with babies—babies having babies.

Each family had a story—many with hope, and others with despair. My nurse Terry and I talked to a lot of social workers from ACS (Administration for Child Services) and wrote many letters in response to the many problems. Many parents were reported by a so-called drop-a-dime call from neighbors or "friends" concerned about the care of their children. In the office we would have to call ACS about what we had observed, heard, or found during an examination in the office. You only have to listen to comedian D. L. Hughely to hear the way some black mothers would talk to their children. Well, I heard mouthfuls of trash coming out of the mouths of some of the more potty-mouthed parents at the office. After a few years I would puff up and tell the mothers, "Please don't talk like that to your child." Even later when I became older and more set in my ways, I would back it up by saying, "I will have to report child abuse if that continues." Word got out that cursing was not tolerated. Most would understand, but then again there were others who felt I was interfering with the upbringing of their child. I asked a few to leave my office, often to the applause or nods of other parents. I am sure I have lost a few patients that way. The majority of the mothers in the practice that I have come to know are kind and good. Some are desperate, but their despair is matched by the ferocity of their love for their children. I have learned a lot in the past three decades. It has been a rewarding experience.

We struggled with the development of the practice for many years, and it grew apace. To help boost the practice and add to its income, I brought in several other doctors: Dr. Beverly Anderson, who worked on

Wednesday and Friday afternoons because many teenage girls preferred a female doctor; a pediatric allergist, Dr. Vincent Hutchinson; and Wiener LeBlanc, who was also the deputy director of pediatrics at Harlem Hospital Center. They all worked either two afternoons or evenings and paid rent. Other doctors—Josef Khakoo, Kwame Yeboa, and Luis Estevez—soon joined the group. Sandy Shepherd, who was on staff at Columbia Presbyterian Meedical Center CPMC was working at the Claremont office. Her house and office on Ninety-Second Street burned down, and she asked me if she could rent time in my office. She was a colorful doctor and had been an activist in the Harlem community for years. She was prominent in assisting young women who had been incarcerated to get out of jail and back on their feet. Unfortunately, she suffered an untimely death after a few years. When Vincent Hutchinson found another office nearer to Harlem Hospital, where he worked, Dr. Tetifyo from St. Luke's came about to take his time slots. Among his patients, he was noted for his economy of words; evidently, he had little to say.

By late fall, I was even able to do some office renovating, thanks to an influx of patients and renewed confidence that I could make a go of my pediatric practice. I agree with the philosopher Hegel, who said, "Life is not made for happiness, but for accomplishment." I finally looked forward to going to the office every day and had become cautiously optimistic about my financial situation. With all the doctors working at both offices, things were working out better and I had to work fewer hours. I could read more books, such as *The Mists of Avalon* and *The Valley of Horses*. However, reality came in the form of an article published on February 12, 1983, in the *New York Times*: "The real income of physicians in the United States has stayed flat for the last decade. Despite a huge increase in the amount of money spent on doctor's services according to the J.A.MA, the average physician's net income in 1979 was $81,900." (This was only $1,400 higher than ten years earlier, the study said—an increase of just 1.7 percent. How well I knew. Nothing changed in five years except the cost of everything.

Practice in Harlem has its differences and moments of great fun as well as some unhappiness. It took a little time to get used to some of the

Ebonics. At first I was so confused. People would say "ammonia" for pneumonia and other things I can't remember.

There were many unique personalities and distressing social problems to deal with. The community of Harlem was then and still is grossly underserved by physicians. Many do not want to practice in Harlem and do not want to have Medicaid patients or welfare problems. It was an interesting challenge.

The Medicaid population suffers from a dependent attitude. They need letters from doctors and social workers to get a step further. I wrote a letter for a woman to get a telephone in her house because her daughters have a history of asthma; but she was using their medical problem to get something that would have been so easy to get on her own.

Young black guys dressed in Bear jackets i.e. Jackets with a big bear face and hoods stood around in the street, on corners, or in front of their brownstone hovels pulling at their penises, spitting, and saying *fuck* thirty times an hour. I wondered what they thought about. Where were they going?

Young black girls, fat and skinny, also wearing the Bear jackets, walked in the busy streets with baby carriages, using the same salacious ten-word vocabulary and smoking joints. They constantly yelled at and threatened their children. They demeaned their girls and ranted at their boys.

Many of the children at the Harlem office are not well behaved. They would constantly wander away from their mothers, exploring; and the mothers did not like my telling them to keep their children in the waiting room. They thought it was perfectly normal for their children to walk up and down the halls and touch and break everything they could. The computer seemed to be an unavoidable attraction, and they sometimes turned off the power when I was working on files. The children reacted violently to getting any tests or immunization. They not only kicked and thrashed about and screamed wildly, but their parents were unable (or unwilling) to control them. The parents were very content to watch *The Jerry Springer Show* and BET videos. I should have asked them how many books they read to their children.

The middle-class black parents were trying hard to raise their children to be better. They were focused. And they were so busy being black; I would ask what they did culturally that was essentially black. I counseled them to think about college tuition for their children, and most had a program in place. Still, I thought the middle-class people in Harlem were less middle class than the middle-class people I knew at Claremont; maybe I was biased. I would have to look into that.

Anecdotes from Harlem

Here is just a sampling of the things I heard from parents and patients at my Harlem practice:

One mother said her child "served six years at school and was walking this year."

Telephone call: "This is Brenda, I had my baby in your office three years ago. Do you remember me?"

"You doan be lassenin' to me."

"Dr. Nichols, you know the deal."

"You sho' took the worryation out of me."

"I want my tubes tied. Do they cut them out, or do they still burn them out?"

One mother was irate because the school took her son to the school dentist without her permission. When she talked to the teacher, she said, "You will have to get a note from your private dentist so that we can be sure that your child doesn't have contagious teeth to contaminate the other children at school."

One woman said her mother told her to cover her baby's face "so the air won't get to it because that's how babies get colic."

I had this conversation with a sixteen-year-old in the clinic:

> "Are you sexually active?"
> "Yes."
> "What sort of birth control do you use?"
> "Nothing."
> "Why? Don't you know she can get pregnant?"
> "Oh, no she can't—I only give it to her in the butt."

In response to the same line of questioning another adolescent said, "Oh, no—we use withdrawal. We do it in the showers, and it all goes down the drain."

"In the hospital they fed my baby by IV through the head."

"Are you feeding your baby cow's milk?"
"No, he gets regular milk."

"I came today because the baby broke out in the same scaly rash he had before. You called it cerebral dermatitis."

"Dr. Nichols, what's that disease people get when they eat each other—syphilis or gonorrhea?"

This weight loss story was told so often: a thirty-four-year-old obese African American [parent came in complaining of early menopausal symptoms (hot flashes, etc.) and high cholesterol. I lectured her on the need for weight loss and made clear what the effects on her knees and heart would be twenty to thirty years later.

I could tell many stories about sons really never leaving their mothers—a boy coming back in his twenties and thirties with a woman who looked and acted like his mother and with a new baby in his arms. A grandmother would be warned jokingly not to touch the baby because the moment she did she would be "hooked", and then the son would ask if she would babysit for one night (which of course would turn into many!).

Grandmothers

I think grandmothers are the backbone of black families. They are so often the caretakers, if not the daytime babysitters. I saw them so often in the practice; they deserve special mention. They had different names: Nana, M'deah, Gramma, Grandmother, Mommom, Grammity, and Grandmama. They taught mothers how to be better mothers and help them to raise their children. A tip that I gave was that they and the other people in the family should teach the parents how to save by buying savings bonds, which were an easy way to provide for the children's education in the future.

The Variety of Patients

The demographics of Harlem have changed so much in my lifetime. In the thirties and forties there were a substantial number of white families, mostly Jewish, living in Harlem. There were small sections of Italian Harlem on the East Side. There were many synagogues, as well as Bernstein's department store, and the Apollo Theater featured Al Jolson and Eddie Cantor. In the thirties the colored population started moving in, beginning with the apartments that became available around 135th Street. By the fifties, there was a majority of colored people—a mix of American colored people and Jamaicans—and enough to elect Adam Clayton Powell to Congress. At present the demographics are changing again. Now there are many white and Asian people living in Harlem. The Old Italian Harlem areas are home to Hispanics, mostly Puerto Ricans. In the late nineteen century and early twentieth century, a huge wave of immigrants from southern Italy and Sicily moved into the areas around Pleasant Avenue in East Harlem, with borders ranging from Ninety-Sixth Street on the south to 125th Street on the north. Now there is a growing number of West Africans, mostly French speaking from Senegal, Mali, and Niger, who have residences below 116th Street.

In my practice I see many African immigrant families. There is also a growing Caucasian population. Hispanic patients form around a quarter of the practice. They are a very mobile population, with many leaving New York for Latin communities all over the United States. They will be a political force in the next twenty years.

The behavior differences between patients and parents at Claremont and those at 139th Street were often obvious. The mothers at 139th Street would often curse, slap, or call their children all kinds of names (like "ugly nigger") in the waiting room. Only very rarely did I see mothers reading to their children or even saying anything to them but commands or derisive comments.

The white, Asian, and "bourgie" black parents from Claremont would be shocked when they came to the office in Harlem. Many said they would not return, and others dropped out of the practice. One of my old friends looked around at the office and the people and asked, "What happened, Ed?"

The Claremont office had people with problems, but these in Harlem were different people. The people in Harlem were more my people, by birth, culture, and history. It was a strange new feeling; I was becoming very racial.

The teacher in me asked the single parents, "Why don't you go back to school?" "Why not get your GED"? "Why not?" I was happily surprised when on subsequent visits they said they had thought about what I had said and planned to go back to school. As time went on, some did, and others—overwhelmed by the events of life—didn't. I was happy to have contributed to those who went back to school.

The middle-class kids at Claremont were frankly smarter, more aware, and more verbal. They seemed to have more of a sense of entitlement too. I always came into the examining room with the avuncular question "Why are you here?" It became a trademark. I asked this question to find out how aware the children were about their presence, just what they were doing in the world.

Their awareness certainly had to do with exposure to things and all, but there seems to be a fundamental difference as well. They would come and sit on the table and chat with me, just like my own noisy girls at home. I sensed that there was more "concerted cultivation" (to use a term from Malcolm Gladwell's *Outliers*) in the homes of the middle-class kids. Gladwell points out that middle-class kids tend to be more alert, poised, attractive, and well dressed. There is a difference between those schooled by their families to present their best face to the world and those denied that experience. Gladwell also says in *Outliers*, "Each of us has his or her own distinct personality. But overlaid on top of that are tendencies and assumptions and reflexes handed down to us by the history of the community we grew up in, and those differences are extraordinarily specific."

I made a point of asking kids in the practice at 139th Street about events and things I hoped they would know—what I thought would be basic questions. "Who is the president?" "What school do you go to?" Most schools have historical names like Joan of Arc, Booker T. Washington, Brandeis (a justice of the Supreme Court), Charles Evan Hughes (another Supreme Court justice), Martin Luther King, Edward W. Stitt, St. Carlos Borromeo, Julia Richmond (first woman superintendent of schools). I would ask "Who were they?" Unfortunately the answers were less than I expected. I guess my grandmother's teaching genes were coming out. I wasn't trying to be mean, but I am at times outspoken when I want to be avuncular, a sort of Dr. Gillespie.

I had a copy of my favorite poem "If—" by Rudyard Kipling and Lincoln's second inaugural address hanging in the office hallway. I would ask some of the more intelligent kids to read it. That revealed another surprising thing: many of the kids could not read at an age-appropriate level. They struggled with words and word comprehension. I put Bill Cosby's book *Come On, People* on the shelf in the waiting room and pointed it out to people to read. Most parents were receptive but often sank back into their daily problems without considering reading the book or thinking about what it was saying. Bill Cosby began giving his presentation of the message in *Come On, People* all over the country with Dr. Alvin Toussaint and started a series of talks with Michelle

Brandon on MSNBC. We need more and more of this. We have to build around these children a community of ambition, achievement, intellectual curiosity, and hope.

Remembering the past is a way in which we can affirm our identity and the value of our own life stories as we grow older. Claiming our stories—with their celebrations and crises—can bring a sense of integrity to our later years.

It occurred to me recently that in the course of thirty-five years of practice I have told so many "my father did this" stories. I practically invented him for my patients. This is a psychological gold mine. I told five- to ten-year-old boys and their parents that my father would hit me in the morning because he "knew that at some time during the day I would be bad." Or I would say that my father would turn off the lights and then hit us in the head so that we could say who hit us, or he would tell us to turn our faces away and then would hit us on the back of the head. Or I would claim, "In the old days we used to get beaten all the time and no one said anything. There was no BCW when I grew up." These stories were to demonstrate how we got disciplined. I boiled it down to "The Nichols School was a hard school."

I certainly stressed education to the kids in the practice. I suppose this came from my grandmother Sylvia being a teacher and graduating from South Carolina Colored Normal School in 1905. I often asked kids about the definition of certain words they used or saw in the office or in the magazines that were in the office. If they didn't know the meanings of the words, I would put a dictionary in their hands and ask them to look them up. I encouraged mothers and fathers to get their kids to use computers—whether at home, in school, or at the library—to find answers to my many questions. My mother gave me a large one-volume encyclopedia to read when I was ten. My "fantasy father" stories came up in this area too. "When I was a kid," I would say, "my father and I would do this and do that." To the boys around ten and eleven who I thought should be more attentive in school I would say often, "Every day you wake up, you should fall on your knees and thank God that I am not your father. I would expect you to learn something new every day." I should never add a quote from Bruce Lee that you can learn from a fool. But the thought is there

Often I would remember my childhood experiences and wonder about not having a father around and how it affected me. On reflection, I can see that it was at those times I wished I had a father present to talk to. I think children—both boys and girls—need fathers. I know how I talked to the girls and heard my speeches echo back to me while they were growing up. I never had any speeches from my father, though. I suppose that was why I talked so much to the kids that came into the practice. I am sure that many did not have fathers around to talk to or to listen to. Again the adage "Physician, heal thyself" comes to mind. It is amazing to think about that now; it brings tears to my eyes. I am sure it had a lot to do with my naiveté growing up, not learning about good and evil until late. There were lots of life lessons that I think only a father could have taught me. Perhaps that is why over the years I have encouraged fathers in the practice to share experiences and adventures with their sons, and talked about the discipline that my father gave us children—knowing full well that none of it was true. It was my fantasy father. "My father didn't say much—he said things once, and then things began to fly. I learned how to duck and run very quickly." I had many anecdotes to tell the young boys.

I talked about the beatings with switches we used to get as kids. I would explain, "They don't use switches here anymore … but for a few dollars parents can take their children to Jamaica, and in the airport there is a big black woman named Elaine who sells switches and can take you and your child to a little room and for five dollars more will show you how to use them. She guarantees it works." The parents would all nod in agreement.

Recently, a young black teenager came in to pick up his school forms to play basketball in school, and I asked him my usual questions about school. Since he was a junior I inquired about the SATs and his prospects for college. He said he was getting all those things prepared. We talked briefly about Obama being president and how different things were from when I was a teenager. There were no Negro bus drivers or motormen or conductors on trains, no Negroes in the construction industry, and very few Negro policemen on the force. He was very shocked to hear this, and I advised him that he should talk to the old black men in his community and in his family and listen to their stories of what life was like when they were growing up. He promised that he would and smiled as he left the office.

Adolescents

I have had many conversations with mothers and their teenagers about the psychodynamics that are in play during this time in their lives. I point out that the adolescent struggle for identify involves a separation from the parent wherein the adolescent finds fault with or is totally against all that the mother says. All this is a process of self-identification. "I know this or that, and you don't." Only later—sometimes much later, when the adolescent reaches eighteen or nineteen—does the struggle wane. This is helped often by the physical separation of college or living conditions such as marriage or the adolescent leaving the house or even going into the service. The adolescent living in the dorm at college hears stories similar (or even more dramatic) about their peer's parents. "I cried because I had no shoes, until I met a man who had no feet"—that sort of thing. "Damn, it could have been worse," they think. This causes a lot of uh-huhs in their minds.

Often, it's only after the late twenties or even early thirties that real reflection takes place and the feelings and memories of adolescence get resolved.

Driving to Work

To get to work, I drive down the Major Deegan, which is lined with weed, dirt, and trash on the shoulders. Lumbering semis and buses race to the many casinos in Atlantic City. Juveniles drive vans, darting thru traffic. Construction often forces traffic into one lane, causing long delays. After passing the George Washington/Cross Bronx interchange, I finally get off at the Macombs Dam Bridge, where young Guatemalans hawk bags of peeled oranges at the traffic light. The old suspension bridge rocks as buses and trucks jump on the other end of this huge metal seesaw. And then I pull into Harlem at 155th Street and swing left onto Seventh Avenue (Adam Clayton Powell Boulevard), driving past the old Dunbar apartments and the newer Esplanade Gardens and then past old tenements that are finally being renovated for occupancy. Most of the stores start to open after eleven o'clock. Harlem awakens slowly and unevenly. People start basking in the sun early. Schoolchildren swarm over broad Seventh Avenue, going to school or running away from school. Grandmothers and steatopygic black ladies push small carriages or strollers with big, fat, babies inside. Old men sit on crates and makeshift chairs against the wall. In the late autumn and winter, there is always a fire going in a barrel. Every Thursday during the summer and early autumn, vegetable trucks from North Carolina bring collards, turnips, string beans, and watermelons in season. Various crazed and drugged people stumble down the streets, mumbling or ranting to themselves or anyone who has the misfortune to see them. Spent old heroin addicts share the sidewalk with new crack heads and various drunks. An occasional Dominican pair yells at each other at close range. A sleek, voluptuous, young black gal high steps to her doom. Young studs already marked for death in the man streets strut along the newly cleaned streets of Strivers. Row. There are no movies being filmed today.

What Happened to the Kids in the Practice?

Many of my early patients have gone on to wonderful professions; they are lawyers, teachers, doctors, and so on. Many have contacted me in the past few years recalling conversations and advice. I see them working in banks and even airline terminals. Some come over to my table at restaurants in the city to say hello. That has been very rewarding. I recently had lunch with Michael and David Brown, who both graduated from Harvard Law School. Mylan Denerstein became the legal counsel for Governor Andrew Cuomo. Many have become police officers, plumbers, and electricians. I am pleased with them all. They often stop by the office and want to say hello. I must confess that I do not recognize many of them as adults. I say that I have had as many patients as there are in seats in Yankee Stadium and it would be impossible to remember all the faces and those of the parents who brought them. But there are several exceptions—the wonderful daughter of Gerry Feagans, Leslie Kyrin Feagans Dunston, who became a professor of obstetrics and gynecology in Savannah is one; and Anu Bhagwati, who became the executive director of Service Women's Action Network, is another.

Chapter Ten

MY DAUGHTERS

My daughters are the light of my life, my raisons d'être. They have become closer still since the passing of Gayle, who left us after suffering for more than five years with Lewy body disease, which is a combination of Alzheimer's and Parkinson's disease. Our closeness goes beyond the group hugs, the cell phone conversations and text messages, the calls when arriving at some new destination after a long flight. Meredith, who is currently doing a Wanderjahr of sorts at different hospitals working as a physical therapist, calls every week. It is the warmth and tone of the contact. We really celebrate Christmas, with a lovely dessert party that they fully enjoy, and have a great Christmas dinner with family and friends. I must confess that I push the dessert party a lot more than they do, but they come through with lots of help and assistance. On Christmas day after we open the presents the girls jump on the paper wrappings and frolic and laugh. I always take pictures of this joyous event.

I won't go all the way back to taking them to pre-K, elementary school, junior high, and then high school, though of course I remember well all the times we went through: their wearing braces, taking riding and dancing lessons, the many trips.

Thursday, Feb. 7, 1985

From Christy ...

Mom, Please tell Meredith to stay away from me, because she is teasing me and I'm trying to keep quiet so I won't bother anyone! I'm not touching or speaking to anyone. You even told me to shut up, so that what I'm doing. you shouldn't expect any noise from me. Just pretend I'm not here. You have been ignoring me and paying more attention to Meredith, but I don't care if you don't invite Michelle and Shawna over. It won't make a difference.

I helped them with their homework where I could in writing and composition, and Gayle helped with math. We practiced Spanish, which they have a working knowledge of now and use in their professions. During the summers they went to various camps, attending swimming camps at the Iona College campus or working as counselors at the Beth El synagogue. I brought them to the office when they were older and showed them how I practice. They even held babies when I examined them or gave them immunizations. They saw some young teenage girls with babies. They had a good time on several occasions, which probably influenced Christy to become a pediatrician. Who knows?

I remember back when they were in college and grad school, when we visited them on their campuses at Cornell, Tufts, University of Rochester Medical School, and the University of Southern California and, naturally, attended their graduations. It was a long, hard financial struggle for me, but it had to be done.

I have recently begun scanning the photos from the many—it must be at least thirty—albums that I have put in the dark and dusty shelves of the den. I relive a lot of the moments in the photos, trips to Canada, Nova Scotia, Italy, Sweden, Mexico, Disney World, and Martha's Vineyard, among other places, over the last twenty to thirty years and remember the faces, the shouts of joy, and the tears of the girls growing up. I have sorted them after many hours of work using the Picasa 2 program on the computer. I intend to make collages and give them as presents on Christmas.

My girls were always noisy and clamoring for attention. Thank God they also liked to either read or write. Christy would read, and Meredith would write about her fantasies. Meredith collected bears of all sizes and colors, and played with them until they ended up looking sad on the shelves and bookcases. They had their quarrels and big sister–small sister issues. But they had many other times when they would squeal with joy. At other times, when they were older, they would wrestle and throw each other around, tripping, falling, screaming, and yelling, barely missing the corners of the wooden table and marble coffee tables. The doctor in me feared all sorts of head and neck injuries.

A few years ago I heard another story from our family history. It seems that, when Christy was twelve, I had obviously had a bad day at the office; I heard of a thirty-five-year old man who had made a twelve-year-old girl pregnant. It must have enraged me. I came home and, according to Christy, pushed her against the wall and grabbed her by the collar and shouted "Don't you ever get pregnant!" She has remembered that to this day. I do not remember this story but will add it to the "Legends of Christy."

Meredith

Meredith is not a child or a name but a force.

We went to Disneyland and Universal Studios in the 1980s and headed toward on the Space Mountain ride. Christy did not want to go on the roller coaster, but we all said it was no big thing. She came with her head hung low. Meredith on the other had wanted to show how brave she was, and she said she would go with me in the front car. We boarded the ride and set off bravely. After the first deep dive and turn. Christy and Gayle were screaming. I was yelling, and Meredith was uncharacteristically silent, gritting her teeth. But she loved the ride and wanted to go again. Christy was just glad she survived. Meredith laughed through all of the rest of the many rides, especially any other roller-coaster ride like Thunder Mountain.

This detail about Meredith comes from a 1984 entry in my diary:

> Meredith has a loud penetrating voice that continues incessantly if unchecked and even thereafter. She commands, explains why she can't do what you want her to do at the moment. She goes on and on until she collapses in a frazzled heap.

This is note is dated September 26, 1984:

Dear Christy
From Meredith Nichols

I was 6 in 1984
I was born in 1978

When I was a little baby I would always giggle. Daddy and you would go to bed and mommy and me would stay up because I had gas. Mommy would always say "Here comes the airplane" when the food was on the spoon. That's what mommy would do. She would do that because I would eat it only that way.

Hey Dad, as interesting as that was. I have to go finish my homework and you have to go to sleep. I also have another softball game. I hope you enjoyed this message but, like every good thing in this world, it has to come an end sometime. Bye love, Me.

This entry is from Tuesday, February 26, 1985:

On Sunday morning, I asked Meredith to set the table for breakfast. She answered O.K., but I have to wake my dolls first!

Meredith always thought Christy got the better version of everything: better Christmas presents, clothes, toys, and so on, but one Christmas she won the raffle at some event or another, and lo and behold, the biggest Christmas stocking I have ever seen came to the house—full of toys, all for Meredith and none that she would share. Christy's head was in a slump, even after I gave her a bunch of other toys. She sat bravely throughout the gift-giving ceremony we have every Christmas, and when it was over, it was over. I got up and asked her to come outside to the garage. There, standing in the front of the garage, was a beautiful, shiny new bicycle. She screamed for joy. I said to her, "Let this be a lesson! Never be jealous of what someone else gets for Christmas." I have always tried to be even handed with them. I always manage to have a surprise present to balance things.

Another time, Meredith was feeding an emu at Busch Gardens on Route 4. She insisted on feeding the bird, who was a naturally mean animal. Meredith put out her hand to give the beast the food, and the emu bit her. She howled. She still remembered the bite when we walked through the San Diego Zoo and ran into the emu's cousin.

Another adventure that could have had tragic consequences happened at the Twin Lakes riding school, where the girls took horseback riding lessons. One fine day Meredith was riding a horse named Diablo, who was having a bad day and decided to roll over and scratch his back—while Meredith was on his back. I saw the horse going down on his knees and shouted in my Daddy voice to Meredith, "Get off the f--ing horse!" Meredith reacted appropriately to the Daddy voice and jumped. Every one there—some twenty people, parents and friends of the children—stood still and watched the excitement. The horse rolled and rubbed the saddle on the stable ground. The trainer ran over to the horse and started to hit the horse and dragged it up, yanking on the bridle. I picked up and hugged Meredith, who was quite frightened.

Meredith and Christy will ride or drive anything; they love surf boarding, windsurfing, ocean kayaking, zip lining, driving dune buggies, riding horses, rock climbing, mountain climbing, and countless other activities. As youngsters at home, both Christy and Meredith both loved sports. And we had all kinds of paraphernalia for the backyard. Shuttlecocks for badminton, horseshoes, croquet sets. I even bought and assembled an outdoor above-ground pool We spent summer nights in a net gazebo, protected from the mosquitoes. As the girls got older and stronger, we had a Sunday morning ritual after Sunday breakfast. We mowed the lawn, which usually took up one and one-half hours. We dumped the clippings in the mulch pit in a far corner of the property. We weeded the garden. "Dad, isn't that enough?" "No, that patch over there needs you." We were exhausted after two or three hours. Gayle served us iced tea or lemonade. Meredith became adept at skirting work, always finding an excuse to go do something else or get something else. She has made that an art form. The garden work ritual was sometimes rewarded with a trip to visit my brother Skippy, who had built a gorgeous pool in his backyard.

Family summer vacation times were also a regular event. One year we headed to Hilton Head in South Carolina for one week. As was always the case when I drove with my two daughters in the backseat of the car, it was an experience I vowed I'd never let happen again. My diary describes it best: "It seems the moment they get into the backseat, the boxing bell goes off in their precious little heads and they come out swinging."

> Round one, begins with: "Move over, you're in my space."
> "No, I'm not," says the challenged. The gauntlet has
> been thrown. Taunts and protests and insults escalates
> until the scene is one of screaming, shoving, hitting,
> laughing and crying. My teeth grind off whatever
> remaining enamel there is after a half century of coping
> with parental reality. My back muscle grip my spine
> and tear at my flesh, sending the hairs into a porcupine
> display. The acid from stomach heads for my heart and
> then settles in my esophagus. I snap. A voice that even
> I don't recognize, howls like a fury possessed, blood
> and madness in the eyes. My bellowing bounces off the
> roof of the car, stunning the banshees in the back seat.
> Through my rear view mirror, wide-eyed stares from
> the now innocent occupants greet me. The shock of the
> sudden outburst lasted for approximately four miles. No
> one dares to speak for fear of waking the beast in the
> front seat. Quiet reigns, the giant brute is calm again,
> in control, focused on the road and the passing scenery.
> Definitely in charge of all who surround him.
>
> Then, from the furthest reaches of the vehicle, comes a
> tiny voice. "Move over, you're in my space," it says, The
> beginning of round two. And we're still hundreds of
> miles from our destination. The beast seethes. He vows
> that this is positively the last such car trip for all time
> and forever more.

At Hilton Head, which is a beautiful resort. I had my first golf lessons and fared rather well with my brother-in-law, Tony, with whom I sweated in the summer heat of South Carolina. We ended up exhausted and frustrated, acknowledging that golf is a game of fitness and determination, not strength.

The week was fraught with other mishaps. Christy got stung by a Portuguese man-of-war while wading in the beach water. It left her with a horrible sting rash on her lower leg, which lasted for months.

One of the last trips I took with the girls was in July 1995. I decided to couple two things: my thoughts about seeing my friends in Italy and showing the girls a part of the world that I held dear. I knew that I would never have another time to share those things with them. They were at the time in their lives when they did not want to be with their father on vacation.

I flew with Meredith from JFK to Rome and then drove up the coast to Grosseto to visit my Swiss friends from Basel, the Egelers, who had bought an old farmhouse in Tuscany. I wanted to see them and what they had done with the old homestead. I met Christoph at the train station. He was wearing an old Yankees baseball hat! He was still the great guy that I had known in Switzerland forty years before.

We drove up into the lovely hill country of Tuscany and the cypress tree–lined roads and finally got to Christoph's beautiful home. He had done an exquisite job of restoring the farmhouse. I am sure he had brought down some of his Italian workers from Basel. The floors were done in red marble, and the huge wooden beams were stained dark. You could look out of the large vertical windows to see the panorama of the Tuscan hills, a very nice place to be.

We spent a lovely week touring the villages and farmland that studded the rolling, hilly countryside and eating lunches and dinners in the many restaurants. Eating in Tuscany is a culinary experience and a wonderful education and excursion for the taste buds. Meredith and I were thrilled.

We went swimming in the Ligurian Sea and then took a day trip to Siena and walked in the Piazza del Campo and took many photos from the tower of the Museo Civico. I especially remember climbing the very narrow staircase.

We later met Christy in Rome and after a day of shopping on the Via Veneto and elsewhere, we took a day trip to Naples and went to see the ruins of Pompeii. The girls were always carping about my going on culture trips, but this one caught their attention. The ruins were spectacular.

We then flew to Sardinia. I had been there with Nicci and Natasha and wanted to share the island with the girls. It was the Fare Augusto, when the entire nation of Italy is on vacation, many of them sunning their gorgeous, thin bodies on the sandy beaches of Sardinia.

Meredith has indeed moved on since those younger years. At thirty-five, she has established herself in Austin, Texas. She has a doctorate in physical therapy from the University of Southern California. She works in a clinic near Austin and has recently returned from a trip to China where she and a team of her colleagues gave lectures on equipment that they use in their clinic to assist patients.

My wife June and I just returned from Austin, Texas, where we celebrated Meredith's marriage to Ben Shook. He is also a physical therapist and loves to brew his own beer. We had a great time with his family and three generations of Shooks, a German American family from Tulsa, Oklahoma.

Christy's Wedding

Christy matured, went to Cornell and then to medical school at the University of Rochester, and finally, started working in my Claremont office near Columbia University. She is now a board-certified pediatrician, having passed her specialty boards late last year. I confess to being very proud of her in spite of my often saying, "I am just happy that she is happy." She is so caring, so concerned, and so aware of the patients' and parents' concerns. We have conferences in the evening after I finish working at the Harlem office and bring over charts and supplies that she will need the following day. We discuss the interesting patients and problems, the abnormal lab tests and the difficult diagnoses she has considered. She says she relies on my forty years of practicing general pediatrics, and I say I rely on her expertise of the new knowledge and acumen in diagnosing difficult and strange diseases.

"Dad," she might say, "we have nine-year-old female who has had symptoms of A.B.C. And D. for x amount of years," and we'll discuss the case and the differential diagnoses. She tells me what studies she has gotten and what she thinks the patient has. It can turn out to be something incredible like eosinophilic esophagitis or ABCD Dx. We do have an interesting balance of expertise. I remind her of the old medical saying, "When you hear hoof beats. you don't think immediately of zebras." But then I remind her of some of the incredible diagnoses that I have made in the past—strange diseases like ectodermal dysplasia and familial Mediterranean fever. We talk about difficult children and even difficult parents and how to react to either of them. I remind her of patients that the nurse practitioner who has worked with me for scores of years has brought to my attention. I do have to remind her to leave the office at the office. She worries about her patients a lot. I suppose we both do.

Christy married Akira Reynaldo Bryson in Kauai on Saturday, May 25, 2008. We had a great week celebrating on a plantation with about seventy of her friends and relatives. We enjoyed a great luau at the Kilohana Plantation as well as barbecues, kayaking, zip lining, surf boarding and more. The wedding itself was spectacular, taking place in front of a giant banyan tree on the beach. In the last four years, Christy has become the mother of a vibrant, beautiful, intelligent four-year-old, Naia Gayle, and another daughter the beautiful and marvelous, Inara Leigh.

Natasha

Looking at the picture of Natasha in my consultation room makes me wonder how she is doing. She doesn't answer my letters but occasionally sends a letter asking me about my family tree, of which there is little information available and about which I have given her all that I know, have heard, or have read. In comparison Natasha has looked up the Sparre family tree, old Swedish nobility from which Nicci and her mother descended. She was so interested in her lineage. I told her that there was movie made of the family Elvira Madigan. The tragic love affair between Elvira Madigan and Count Sixten Sparre in 1889 was depicted in a film in 1967 with music from Mozart's Piano Concerto No. 21 in C, K. 467. There are books listing all the nobility of Europe, and Nicci and her family are in it. Natasha is more in contact with her half-sisters Christy and Meredith, with whom she exchanges photos and short messages now and again. Natasha writes about her travels with her long-time boyfriend and significant other Bjorn. We do get cute Christmas cards that she has drawn.

Dear Natasha,

As I wrote you by email. I was excited and happy to read your letter. Yes I too would like to talk to you and tell you who and what I am. Perhaps it would clear the air and let some light on many things. I was surprised to read that you didn't get word of Gayle's illness and demise. I thought you knew how ill she was, and the details of her problem. I am further surprised that you and the girls never discussed it. Gayle suffered a long four years of dementia preceded by many years of failing health. She had many health issues and many that were not understood by any of us at the time. Looking back it was similar to what her father had succumbed to. The Porters filled us in about her father Kline and we all said Oh that is what was going on. Her last years were difficult to deal with. But she had 24/7 care and finally died. The girls and I lived through this and have bonded even more because of it.

As far as you are concerned, we all had and have wished you to come to New Rochelle for many years. We all wanted you to be part of the family. Attempts at contact with me were all rebuffed, contact with the girls seemed to be warranted only around Christmas. We talked about you frequently and always hoped to see and be with you. We love you very much.

Being 72 and walking is a pleasure. I have serious medical problems but I am dealing with them as best I can. Diabetes, Hypertension, and now Macular Degeneration (an eye problem) afflict me and I see doctors all the time.

Christy is seven months pregnant and we are looking forward to seeing the baby girl in October. We recently had a big baby shower which brought out the family. Skippy and I even took a picture together.

Yes we are all now Obamistas and wish him well governing this massive country with all the different factions competing with each other. Racism still exists and makes headlines throughout the world. Europeans cannot understand that their Racism against different peoples Africans in France, Spain and Italy and the Slavs and Gypsies is just as bad. We are a much different more diversified country than when you were born. I would love to know just what your mother thought of racism when she was here. She never expressed it to me. I always remember when my mother intentionally drove Nicci and I through Harlem when we arrived in New York. Nicci never told me how she felt. She never spoke her mind about racism. I imagine only that she didn't want to live here or bring you up in this world. I don't think she understood the growing pains of being a doctor and expected something different. I also wondered how you felt about living in the USA. You seemed to be violently opposed to any discussion about living or going to school in the USA. You were also not interested in going to school in Switzerland as Ursula proposed. I remember your outbursts in Rio, Mallorca, Bornholm over the years. It must have been a difficult time for you. I sort of lost hope for any reconciliation after Bornholm and have backed off any contact. You and Nicci found fault with any idea or thought I had.

I certainly would like "to sit on a rock" and talk with you on any subject. Feel free to write and communicate in any way you would like. I certainly invite you to stay a while in New Rochelle. I am almost fully retired so my finances are not permitting me to gad about too much. I do manage to go to Barbados once a year but that is all.

So I will end here hoping to hear from you. Thanks for the pictures of you and Bjorn. You both look fit and happy. Who all were playing at the Jazz Festival?

Love, Dad

I would get occasional letters from Nicci, easily recognizable from the stylized German script she used. The themes of the letters were mostly of sadness, depression, disease, and questions of old age. They were difficult to respond to, sometimes causing arguments that would last for years.

"It is a wise father that knows his own child." So observed Shakespeare in *The Merchant of Venice*. I took his suggestion to heart in 1992 when in August, after a fairly uneventful first half of the year—even the trip to Epcot Center for Christy's seventeenth birthday was pleasant—I took a "vacation" trip to Sweden. The main reason I went was to find out what was going on with my thirty-year-old daughter, Natasha. Her mother, Nicci, along with Natasha herself, had been telling me some very upsetting news via telephone for the past year. It had to do with Natasha's state of—for lack of a better word—invalidism. I was told that she was up and out of bed for only four hours a day, not able to read or draw at all. She was having dizzy spells, migraine headaches, and neck spasms and was constantly fatigued. She had had a traffic accident some years before and suffered post whiplash syndrome. She had seen so many doctors, chiropodists, masseurs, and acupuncturists in the years since then, all without any relief of her symptoms. She had stopped her studies as a graphics illustrator and had been living on the welfare system of Sweden, augmented by money from her insurance claim. I decided to see the situation firsthand and try to get to the bottom of her invalidism in an effort to help her in any way I could—even with the knowledge that typically, whatever I offered to do or however I diagnosed her problems, Natasha would undoubtedly reject my help or suggestions for treatment. But I was so concerned about her, and braced for the worst, that I just decided to go to Sweden and face the situation head on. It couldn't be worse than hearing the escalating bad news on the phone and feeling totally helpless and clueless.

I took both Christy and Meredith with me. Because of Natasha's difficult temperament, I hoped that Christy might bring some balance to the situation, especially since she was in good spirits, having just successfully completed a leadership program at the Wharton School of Economics in Philadelphia. Funded by American corporations, the course was designed to instill leadership qualities in young minority students. Christy did very well in the program, and I was sure it would prove its worth in whatever career she chose after college.

Two hours before we left New York, Natasha called and said she felt well enough to go with us to the Island of Bornholm off the coast of Sweden where I had a traded a time-share to go for a week. She had had her doubts about if she was physically up to the trip. She asked if her boyfriend, Bjorn, could join us. I guessed that she needed his support, and I agreed, as I thought there was a chance it meant her health was improving.

Bodanas, the name of the family estate where Nicci lived, still looked the same. It was six hundred acres among the pine trees in the lake-studded district lowlands of Småland in southern Sweden. The terrain is very reminiscent of Minnesota, which is why so many Swedes settled in the state when they migrated to the United States in the late 1800s.

The manor house, situated on the huge Bodanas lake, was used by the nobility and royalty for many years. The property included a large hunting lodge that had belonged to Queen Catherine of Sweden a century before. The house was filled with museum-quality tapestries hanging on the walls. The manor had many Danish commemorative plates, as well as memorabilia of all those who came to hunt and fish there. Every year, Nicci's mother, Ursula Graefin von Kanitz, made a few restorative changes to the house, but it had not lost a single bit of its charm and elegance. And scenically, it was a beautiful retreat. One had to endure the extremes of weather and of the seasonal extremes of light and dark, though, and it rained frequently. I seemed to always forget that Scandinavian summers last for about two short weeks in July before it starts to get cold again during the nights in August. There is the midnight sun in summer, which means the sun is out, or at least it is completely light, at midnight. The Swedish love this time of year because of all the daylight. In fact, it is too much daylight, at least for me; I find it strange and unsettling. I like sunsets in summer at around eight o'clock and sunrise around six in the morning. There's a nice balance to those hours. But in Sweden at this time of year, dusk sets in at around three thirty in the morning, and then by four thirty, the sun is coming up again!

Unfortunately, the many extra hours of summer midnight sun are reversed during the winter, which becomes a long, dark, depressing affair with barely a hint of sunshine. Winters, which start with fog, cold, and rain and then escalate to snow and ice, begin in mid-October and end in mid-May. The lack of sunshine and the dark cold nights explain on one hand the high suicide rates in Sweden and the sun-worshiping character of the Swedes. Many are "penguins," going south to Mallorca and the Canary Islands. I cannot fault them for that.

When we arrived and settled in at Bodanas, the girls and Natasha and I went for long walks in the beautiful woods and picked lingo berries and mushrooms. We watched Ulf, Nicci's younger brother, and his friend Michael as they laid out the traps on the lake for the huge catches of prawns. During the first week of August there is a feast (the feast of Saint Lucia) to celebrate—what else?—the long days of almost constant light. The feast themselves are wonderful eating and drinking events— prawns cooked in huge vats with flavored salt, fresh lake trout and pike, a meat course (usually roast beef), potatoes, vegetables, and salad, all washed down with beer or aquavit. That summer there were about twelve people at the table, and after the hearty meal was consumed, most of the young and hearty are supposed to jump in the cold waters of the lake. We did this in earlier years but no longer. I was happy to be in Sweden that evening and kept hoping that my visit would continue without unpleasant incident.

Although at first Natasha seemed happy to see us, I noticed that she looked much older and decidedly thinner, which worried me. She had suffered post whiplash syndrome from a car accident two years before, in which she'd been rear ended, and it had apparently left her so weak and generally disabled that Nicci had taken to spoon feeding her while Natasha lay on the couch. Some days she would be up and walk with us in the woods; other days she'd complain of dizzy spells and painful neck spasms and would become so fatigued that she couldn't stand or sit up for more than two hours at a time. This was the history that I was confronted with. I didn't believe it. I was convinced there was something else going on. Perhaps being a doctor made me look for answers.

I talked about Natasha with her grandmother, Ursula, whom I dearly loved. She was somewhat frail by then and wearing a pacemaker, but she still remained amazingly strong in character. She told me that when Nicci and Natasha first came back to Bodanas, Ursula had always wanted to send Natasha off to private schools in Sweden but Nicci had vehemently protested this. Nicci had never made any attempt to leave Bodanas once she and I were divorced and she had moved back to Sweden. Now, years later, of course, she was obsessed (perhaps that is somewhat unkind) with taking care of what she considered her invalid daughter. In the almost two years following the onset of Natasha's condition, she had been to various doctors, chiropractors, masseurs, and even an acupuncturist, but apparently nothing had helped. Nicci wanted me to talk to the doctors who had been treating Natasha. "They won't talk to me because I'm a woman," Nicci said sarcastically. And so, two days into my visit, I went with Nicci to see Dr. Elsa Ingesson at her office in a rehabilitation center in Nässjö, where for two and a half hours we talked about Natasha. She told me that Natasha had been offered sterile water injections, which she considered the best cure for her condition. Although I think it's mostly a placebo effect, the sterile water is supposed to activate our bodies' endorphins, the brain chemicals that produce a healing and pain-relieving result (much like acupuncture, in my line of thinking).

In any case, Natasha refused this treatment, so we'll never know if it would have helped or not. She had also been seen by neurosurgeons and orthopedic specialists. She been given Valium in the past and apparently had had an adverse reaction to it; she said it made her "confused," so she stopped taking the medication. In talking to Dr. Ingesson, I thought she had tried a few appropriate analgesics and nonsteroidal inflammatory medications and treatments, but Natasha was not improving.

The next day I had another visit with Dr. Ingesson, this time with Natasha; Nicci objected, as she did not like or agree with the doctor. When Dr. Ingesson asked Natasha what it was she wanted to get out of the prescribed therapy, my then thirty-year-old daughter broke down in sobbing tears. The doctor told me (when we were alone) that she felt the best thing for Natasha would be to leave Bodanas—even suggesting that Natasha return to America—but at least get treatment somewhere else and grow up. What an excellent evaluation and therapy, I thought. That is really what it's about: Natasha is the dependent, immature child of a mother who is enabling her to be this way. Codependency at its worst.

After my visit with Dr. Ingesson, and over the vehement arguments of Nicci, Natasha relented and said she would take the medicine prescribed and possibly the sterile water injections to relieve the neck spasms. And maybe she would even come to America. I was happy to hear this; so were Christy and Meredith. I think they genuinely liked Natasha and felt a certain closeness, for despite the years and the geographical distances between them, they were, after all, half-sisters. That evening at Bodanas, we all finally relaxed and enjoyed a lobster dinner, complete with a Persian rice pilaf made with saffron, which perfectly complemented the lobsters.

Within a day of Natasha taking some of the pills that I had brought with me and had told Natasha that my surgeon friend Danne Lorieo had recommended, she began feeling much better. In fact, she said, "I haven't felt this good in years." I was so glad that the Motrin worked! She also was using Vicks VapoRub on her neck and an ethyl chloride spray. We decided, thanks to her improved condition, that we could all take the little trip to the Danish island of Bornholm in the Baltic Sea. I commented in my diary about her sudden well-being: "I was relieved to see that it had taken only a few tablets (Motrin) to get Natasha back into shape. I wonder how much was due to just leaving Bodanas?"

We spent a lovely time on Bornholm at an old hotel that had been turned into a time-share. Bornholm is a small granite island situated sixty kilometers off the southern tip of Sweden in the Baltic. The villages are very clean and well kept. There are small farms and rolling hills to bike on. The beaches have fine white sand. The water is too cold to swim in, but we did sit out on the beach chairs. We toured the round Templar churches and had a great time. Four days later, still taking the medicine I had given her, Natasha announced that she now felt fine. She was up the entire day, not needing a rest every few hours, and giving orders to everyone and pouting when she didn't get her way. This led both seventeen-year-old Christy and me to conclude that Natasha was certifiably full of shit—that is, her symptoms were far less that she'd been making of them and she had been manipulating everyone. I began to feel that she was using her illness to hide from the reality of her life. She didn't earn money and had none of her own. She didn't finish her school exams. She was getting financial aid from the state and probably some from medical insurance. I didn't like her infantile behavior at all, but I wasn't about to get into a confrontation or make accusations that would only lead to yet another angry estrangement. Besides, we were on vacation.

The next day, Friday, when we had dinner, I asked Natasha what her plans were. She suddenly bolted, ran off, upset and mad at my question. I asked about the possibility of her not staying in Bodanas and coming to New Rochelle. Ironically, the following morning, all was forgotten. Her boyfriend Bjorn, who had come for support, had run after her and brought her back. Natasha was happy again, laughing, and we all went to the local driving range where Bjorn helped me with my gold swing. In the afternoon, he and Natasha watched as Christy, Meredith, and I rode large Danish horses at the Langholt riding school in Ro. We galloped madly through the woods and dashed along the roadside, with me happily hanging on—madness at my age.

I wasn't surprised when, after being there ten days, when talk got around to returning home to Bodanas, Natasha started to complain that her muscles were weak again, and she had to lie down frequently. Back at Bodanas, Natasha seemed a bit better than before we had left and said the Motrin she was taking had definitely helped. I also knew she was happy with her boyfriend Bjorn, who was a graphic cartoon illustrator and had recently produced some successful cartoon films and, from what I could see, was equally happy with Natasha. But it was Nicci who would continue to influence and in many ways, control my daughter. Nicci was so depressing and excessively emotional, and both trains played right into Natasha's internal insecurity and physical frailty. And so, when I suggested once again before leaving, that it would be a wonderful idea if Natasha could spend some more time with me in Berlin where I was headed before going back to the States—or with her Uncle Andreus, who lived there—it was no surprise that Nicci said absolutely not. Natasha had to be where her mother could keep a close and possessive eye on her. And that was the end of that discussion.

I put the girls on their flight back to New York where Gayle would meet them at the airport. And I took the short flight to Berlin.

Chapter Eleven

DISCOVERING THE DOCUMENTS

October 2, 1994, was the fateful day that Skippy discovered the suitcase containing our parents' correspondence from the 1940s, during World War II, when Leon Terrenze Nichols was in the armed services.

It was also the first time I had seen my father's social security number and could plan to contact the Social Security in hopes they'd be able to provide me with further information. I was certainly excited about the prospect.

Skippy was far less excited. He had never cared as much as I had about going in search of our father. He had, as far as I could understand, reconciled Leon's abandonment of us a long time ago, or perhaps—and I don't mean this to sound coldhearted—he never was deeply affected by it in the first place. We all deal with our hurt and loss in very different ways. I had never found consolation or closure when it came to my father's whereabouts, why he left us, what his life had been like since then, what he was like, and who he was. I had always had a burning desire to know. Skippy may simply have chosen not to let it affect him emotionally, so after so many years, the discovery of Leon and Maude's letters was more of an oddity to him than anything else. Although he knew that finding the correspondence would thrill me, his reaction was pretty much, "Well, I'll be damned—look what we found."

And so, I left Skippy's that day feeling as though I'd moved a small step closer to some of the big changes that were coming in my life, no matter how welcome or unwelcome they might be.

I was still wondering about the fears of my Uncle Roy that I would be opening a "can of worms". Roy Stalnaker, Aunt May's Husband, would frequently walk from his apartment on 92nd street and third avenue, to have conversations with me at my office in Harlem. Often, he would tell me he wanted to "set the record straight", but only just warned me that there might be things I would not want to know about my father and the Atkinson family. I always replied that I still have to know. He would reluctantly sigh and say "Ok.".

On Saturday morning, October 29th, 1994, I found what would be an important part of the puzzle in my mailbox. The death certificate for Leon Terrenze Nichols was sent from Snohomish Health Center in

Everett, Washington. The social security number was almost the same as the one I had for him, but the birth date was off by some fifteen years! It said he was born in 1918, which made him seventy at the time of his death—due to complications from diabetes—not eighty-four, as we had calculated based on the 1903 date of birth that we had on record. It also stated that he was born in Colorado and had the same occupation of auto body repair that we'd always known about, and that his last address was in Everett, Washington. It also stated his father's name was Thomas Terrenze Nichols and his mother was Margarita Rodriguez. The informant was Philip Nichols, living in Mukilteo, Washington. I realized that this meant he had other children and had probably married again, possibly committed bigamy, illegally changed his social security number at least once, and lied about his date of birth—whatta guy!

I called my brother Skippy and told him I'd just received the death certificate. At last we had a real lead. Skippy sounded genuinely excited by the news, and I was pleased that he wanted to find out whatever further information there was. I think he wanted to be the one in charge, which was fine with me.

Within a few days, Skippy phoned. "Come on over tonight," he cheerfully invited me. "I've got some astounding news." Skippy wasn't being overly dramatic; he just wanted to share it with me in person. I knew it would be worth it. That night, I was so intrigued, I went straight form my office to Skippy's home in Scarsdale. And it was one of those rare times when I was so excited, I completely forgot about eating dinner.

We sat in his living room, with its lovely garden view and fine furnishings. Skippy smiled and began, "I called the number for the address on Leon's birth certificate, and an Asian (Japanese) woman answered the phone. She screamed out that she knew Leon T. Nichols and that 'HE WAS A MAN WITH NO PAST AND WAS A LIAR.' She yelled the word *liar* so loud, I had to hold the phone away from my ear!"

Skippy let out a laugh, and I shook my head in disbelief. Neither of us, however, was surprised by this revelation. The woman told Skippy that our father had never talked about his past, and when Skippy asked who Philip Nichols was (the name listed on the death certificate as next of kin), she said he was her ex-husband, a policeman on the force in Everett, Washington, and that she had had little contact with him since their divorce.

Skippy said, "I called all the precincts in Musketilo and Everett and finally located a Philip Nichols in the south precinct of Everett. We had a good talk for a couple of hours. And then he gave me the phone number for his older brother, Harry, who lived in California."

"You mean we have two half brothers?!" I said, sounding shocked but not at all that stunned, really. I guess I was happily surprised to find we had more family.

Skippy nodded, "Yes, we do. And we also have a half-sister." That dropped like a bomb.

"What?!" I replied.

"Her name's Heidi," Skippy said, reading from a legal pad containing the notes he'd made during the phone conversations with our siblings. "She lives in Mount Vernon, up in Washington State. She's thirty-seven, and Harry's fifty. And, are you ready for a bit of news?"

"I don't think so," I said, half laughing.

"Well, it seems Leon never told them about any of us—or any part of his past. The only thing he said was that he was run out of New York City by the Mafia!" I roared at this piece of dramatic history that Leon had obviously fabricated. But then Skippy remembered when he once worked briefly for an Oldsmobile dealership (this was before he studied to be a doctor) and found out that several men who had worked there wanted to find Leon because he apparently owed them money; they were just about ready to send a Mafia wiseguy to kill our father. So maybe Leon hadn't exaggerated after all. But it was certainly the beginning of his double life, or rather, the start of a completely new life accompanied by a successful effort to erase his past.

According to Skippy, Harry and his sister, Heidi, both seemed genuinely pleased to hear from him, and wanted all of us to get together—a long-lost family reunion, you might say.

What was particularly interesting was that she and her brothers did not know that their father was black. He had apparently passed! Their mother was a white woman (of Pennsylvania Dutch ancestry) named Dorothy Winter. She had died in 1970 of cirrhosis of the liver.

But then the news turned horrible, ugly, and depressing. Leon Terrenze Nichols was a drunk, they said, a mean drunk. Philip, Heidi, and Harry's memories were of an alcoholic, abusive father beating their mother. In fact, both Harry and Philip had left home when they were nineteen years old. Their mother, Dorothy, had also been an alcoholic, which was why she had died of liver disease at the very young age of forty-five. Leon had then married another woman, also white, named Virginia Lundquist (this was in the nursing home much later), but they divorced and had no children (at least, that's what we were told).

Heidi told Skippy she doubted that we—Skippy and I—would have ever gotten the education we did and gone on to become doctors, if we had been burdened with the Leon Nichols we never knew, the drunken, violent father that she bitterly remembered.

"Better the father you don't know than the father you do know," I said to Skippy, who nodded solemnly. He agreed with me when I concluded that Maude's efforts to conceal Leon's whereabouts were undoubtedly meant to protect us from his malevolence.

Skippy also told Heidi, Philip, and Harry that he had always thought Leon was black. They said they had been told that they were of German descent. They mentioned having a photograph of their grandfather standing by a fence in front of a large building, which they thought was taken in a concentration camp in Germany. Skippy told them we had the same picture and it was taken in front of our public school in the Bronx. Skippy also told Harry, who was born in 1945, that Maude and Leon were never legally divorced, which of course meant that Leon was also a bigamist, along with his other deceptive practices. In fact, I told Skippy that maybe they ought to contact the state of Nevada just to see if Leon and Maude were actually divorced when he married Dorothy.

Later that evening, Skippy took out a photograph album to show me the pictures of our grandfather, Thomas in front of the public school in the Bronx. There were two ladies standing next to him that Skippy remembered as grandfather's wife Margarita and Maude. Well, at least we knew that Leon and Maude did marry, and I had the marriage certificate to prove it. It was dated May 17, 1933, and we knew that Skippy was born on December 14, 1933 (we were told he had been premature).

Skippy had promised to send photographs of him and me to Philip, Heidi, and Harry, and they all said they'd do the same. We also offered to share some of Leon's early letters with them. And just to absolutely confirm that our father definitely was the same man who fathered these three other people, Skippy had asked Harry if Leon had an amputation of his right index finger. He did! What's more, Harry remembered a quarrel that Leon had had with Dorothy in 1956 over a woman named Maude.

And so, my uncle Roy was wrong. It wasn't a whole can of worms that Skippy and I had opened up. It was the solving of a thirty-year mystery, and it closed a chapter of our lives that had more than its share of tragicomedy.

I told Skippy this was probably the beginning of exchanging visits with our West Coast relatives, and I thought it would be really interesting to get to know them. What were they really like? What was the effect of genetics and nurturing? What if we had all gotten to know each other much earlier?

Two days later, I called my brother Harry, and we talked for two and a half hours. He said that they knew nothing about our father prior to 1944, and I told him that we knew nothing about him after 1944! We figured out that our father was still legally married to Maude when Harry was born. As he grew into an adult and after Leon died, Harry had no desire to find out whether his father and my mother had ever officially been divorced. He did say that he and Philip were born prematurely, each weighing only two pounds. In those days, their survival was very questionable, and poor Philip had to be hospitalized (probably with respiratory distress syndrome) for two months after his birth.

Harry remembered the many episodes of drunken mischief and abuse his parents engaged in as well as the outdoor fun and sports that took place when he was a boy. He also recalled how much moving around they did, from Montana to Idaho to Oregon, all when Harry was only in the fifth grade. It seems they had to be constantly on the move, running from Leon's numerous creditors. Ironically, he eventually struck it rich when he opened up a large chicken ranch with five or six chicken brooding houses in California. He was selling ten thousand chickens a month, but his new wealth soon dissipated when the unions muscled in and put him out of business.

There were times when Harry questioned his father about genealogy, and this was when Leon said he was born in Stuttgart, Germany, and his ancestors were named Wasserleben. But in fact, Leon had been born in Trinidad, Colorado, and later moved to Pueblo. His own father, Thomas, had been a layman in the local Episcopalian Church at the time.

Harry and I danced around the color issue for a long time. I gave him a capsule history of our genealogy on our mother's side, saying that Maude and her friends were "high yellows." (Actually, Mother Maude's grandfather was an African named Friday Kershaw, who became a reverend in the Baptist Church and married a Cherokee woman named Christina Saunders; they had eighteen children, the last of which was my grandmother Sylvia, who married Fred Atkinson. They produced three children: my mother, Maude; her brother, my uncle Edward Atkinson; and my aunt Mae.)

I told Harry that my mother had passed for white, and that we always thought our father was some racial mix with Spanish blood because of the way he looked and the fact that my grandmother had often derisively referred to him as "the Mexican."

He asked me what I looked like, and I said, "Brown on brown on brown," and that Skippy was fairer than me. I told him that both wives were white and my daughters looked white.

Harry said his wife, Delores, was half Mexican, half Swedish and that Philip had been married to a Japanese woman. So I guess we are all still mutts.

Both Harry and I promised to keep in touch, exchange photos, and get together one day to hug each other.

That night, I also called Heidi, but she wasn't home. I then phoned Philip, who was expecting my call. How different he was from Harry. He was a quieter, more spiritual man, who tried to reflect on the positives and negatives of growing up with our father. During the conversation, I heard him almost excuse Leon's excesses of child and wife abuse, drunken driving, and job failures. Philip did admit that Leon's terrible behavior (could there have been a worse role model?) had obviously had an effect on his marriage. In reading between the lines of what he was saying I think our father had made some advances or remarks to Philip's wife that had led her to hate him with the kind of venom that Skippy had heard when he telephoned her.

In any case, Philip did seem to have quite a bit of insight into alcoholism, its stages, and its manifestations, and unquestionably, he was far more forgiving than either Harry or Heidi about Leon's condition and behavior. Philip said that when Harry had left home at nineteen, he didn't reappear for twenty-three more years! It must have taken Harry that long to get rid of Leon's ghosts. It made me think hard about the possibility of how different it might have been for Skippy and me if our father had been present in our lives, and what a mess he might have made of them. We will never know, but certainly his absence had a profound effect.

Chapter Twelve

DISCOVERING THE WESTERN NICHOLS:

My Other Brothers and Sister

We continued our telephone conversations, and exchanged letters and photos. They were shocked to learn that we thought our father was black and expressed consternation to find out they we were black. I sent them pictures of me, and they were shocked to see the similarities between my father and me. One of the reactions to "You know our father was black" was "What, you mean black as in Negro?!" Delores, Harry's wife, laughed and said, "I told you he was black."

I received a letter from my half-brother Philip detailing a brief history of his own life, mentioning some of the things that he had told me when we talked on the phone—how they had moved so many different times, how in one particular community where they had lived they had been surrounded by "rednecks."

Philip had joined the navy to get away from his father, only to be discharged under a hardship situation when his mother Dorothy died. Philip had married his Japanese girlfriend (the one who had screamed about Leon on the phone when Skippy called that first time), and he had two daughters with her. But Philip and Chikako had terrible marital problems, and Philip also drank. He finally did get some treatment, but I realized that the genetics of alcoholism were so dominant in our family. Philip told me that he had diabetes. I was flabbergasted to hear that since I had been diagnosed with diabetes in 1990 and was taking the same medications he was. We were both undone and shaken by this development. It turns out that Leon, our father, had died of complications of diabetes. What a bummer!

Here is Philip's letter in its entirety:

> "Hi! My name is Philip Noel Nichols. This is my story. Some may think its not much of a story, but its the only one I have. Noel is Leon spelled backwards. No I'm not the devil's child, although, sometimes I thought he was my father.
>
> I was born at 1347 hours on May 6, 1947. I was born in St. Mary's Hospital in Modesto, California. It was one of the few times in my life that I've been early. Four weeks early! Sometimes when you are early, they call you names. Names like "preemie" or "Oh! he's so cute," stuff like that. I don't remember any of it but I'm sure that's how it happened.
>
> Dad's name was Leon Terrenze Nichols. He was born on Christmas Eve. I think he was feeling pretty witty and full of Christmas Spirit. That's why he named me "Noel." (Very Christmas Spirit, huh?) My mother's name was Dorothy Phyllis Nichols, formerly Winters. Three years before I arrived my brother Harry Stephen Nichols was born. My coming was probably no big deal to him. I'm pretty sure he didn't like me much cause I was cuter than he was. As we grew up he was O.K. unless he was around girls. He'd get weird and not want to play with me.
>
> I don't remember much of my early years, just bits and fragments of memories. We lived in California when I went to the first grade. I got A's in silly and C's in

behaviour. What saved me was: I was still cute, long curly hair, skinny and a grin that was impossible to wash off my face. I remember Dad raising chickens, Harry starting a fire and a tree swing. Life was O.K. There was a place called glass beach in Fort Bragg, California. I fell in love with the sea as only a four year old can. Then we moved away.

We moved often. I can't really remember some of the places. I think it was Moscow, Idaho, where I went to the second grade. My teacher's name was Mrs. Tuttle. (They modelled Godzilla after her.) Dad worked at a body and fender shop. I used to trade him pennies for dimes so I could buy candy. I got into trouble at school for helping defend the honour of a friend. Even at an early age I championed the down trodden. Teachers and principals don't understand these things. It was my first experience with corporal punishment! You know, to this day, I won't bend over and grab my ankles. Dad understood! Mom was angry! Good little boys don't stuff other children into trash cans. I had to repeat the first grade. Or was it the second?

Time passed and we moved to Kalispell, Montana. I liked Kalispell. Third and fourth grades went O.K. No fights and only 3 stitches above my left eye learning the difference between a baseball bat and my head. Kalispell was wonderful! Floating down the river on inner tubes, fishing, sledding, ice skating, catching trout out of the pond behind the house, playing with my friends, forest fires, growing up! Dad was raising more chickens and working in and out of body shops. Harry discovered older girls and lost his memory about having a younger daughter. She was thirteen and I was ten. Dad had an accident—broke his arm! It was the other guy's fault. Never mind the fact that he had one or two beers himself. Since he couldn't work, he must have played with Mom some, 'cause one day we were told the stork story. Special delivery named Heidi Kay Nichols. So much for freedom. Baby-sitting came first. 1957—time to grow up. Life went on. The fire was scary!!! Ever see a fire truck go by, lights and siren, only to watch it stop at your house? WOW!!

Let's see, moving again—back to Idaho. A place called St. Mary's. A house on the river, a tire swing and the fifth grade. No problem! Dad had a job at the Chevy dealership. I had a new friend. But, something is different. There is a sense of not fitting in. I'm 11 years old, tall, skinny and there is a novelty called team sports. Trust me—I want to fit. But since I'm new, it's like chickens when they see a spot on another chicken— they pick at it. Looking back I think St. Mary's had "redneck" Dads with "redneck" kids. The St. Joe river was deep and green. I liked my friend but Chucky Chase and his crowd could all drown as far as I was concerned. Dad worked for Chase Chevrolet!

Time to move again. Pasco, Washington. Twelve years old, McLaughlin Junior High School and Mary Fast! There was fishing, sports, my best friend—Al Reining and Mary. I tasted hard liquor for the first time. Dad and Mom didn't do very well at remembering how much they drank, so they made me the bartender! Seemed O.K. at the time. Mary was the first girl that I kissed on the lips! It made me dizzy! Fifteen years old and learning to drive. My first date and Dad was driving! Life is NOT fair.

Time to move. Let's try Sedro Wooley, Washington. No, Everett. No, Lynnwood. Wait! Wait! Stop! We lost Harry!!! Where is Harry? Seems when we left Pasco, Harry was out working and we forgot to tell him we were leaving. (That's Harry's story. You'll have to ask him how he felt when he returned to Pasco and found that his family had moved.)

Let's see, where are we now? Let's call it the Everett area. New friends, a driver's license, high school, track, football and 1966. Time to graduate. A great revelation—we are not really gypsies. We just move a lot!!! Christmas Eve, 1966, Lynnwood, Washington on December 24 ... (Dad's birthday). Domestic violence takes on an added dimension. As a gift, I spare his life and think to myself, "time to leave."

Hello—US Navy! Time to protect and serve. What irony! I'm back in California. Isn't this where it all started? I liked the service. Leaving Heidi was the worst!!! I'm bright, smart, and rank comes easily. This is fun. I'm a Petty Officer, 2nd Class. Traveling, protecting, serving! So I drink to go to sleep, so what. Hawaii, yes! Japan, you bet!

Look at her! She is beautiful. Her name is Chikako Mukai. She's Japanese. She talks a little funny but she sure is nice. Now comes the interesting part—she is dating my buddy, not me, but that's O.K. He's married but she doesn't need to know that. Let's see what happens. I know she's asked about him but I need to stay out of this. I shouldn't interfere. I really like her and wouldn't want to see her feelings hurt. It will all work out. Besides, it's 1969. Viet Nam is my next address.

Wouldn't you know it! Dad and Mom have a way of upsetting my plans. The Captain received a telegram from the States saying that Mom is sick and dying. He asked me what I wanted to do: Go home or go to Viet Nam? Viet Nam, I said. Now look at me, I'm on a plane to Seattle. Life is NOT fair. Hardly any time to say good-bye to Chikako. This is not pleasant. I don't want to be back. How can I get away? I know! I'll do what Dad does. All I need to do is stay drunk until this is over. Mom's death was a blur. My feelings were a mess and life "sucked"! I'm 22 years old. Heidi is 12.

Now what? The Navy is willing to help. They call it a Hardship Discharge under Honourable circumstances. I'm out of the Navy, without a mother, my little sister needs help and I don't trust Dad to handle any of it.

Re-enter Chikako. We had exchanged addresses and were writing to each other. Mind you, we didn't really know each other. The only "logical" thing to do was to ask her to marry me. Never mind, that in my wildest dreams, did I think that she would say yes. October 11, 1970, we were married in Marysville, Washington. A few friends and well wishes. We needed more. Just prior to getting married, one of the people who helped comfort me became pregnant. Her friend knocked on the door one day and proudly announced that I was the father of twin girls. (Stacey and Jennifer were born February 21, 1971.) Things between Chikako and me are off to a great start! Chikako had an immediate negative reaction to Dad that never went away. A dog and cat would have been more friendly. No effort, no skill that I applied to make things work had any appreciable effect. I pulled lumber at a Weyerhaeuser mill. Chikako worked at the state employment agency. September 5, 1972, I was hired by the Snohomish County Sheriff's Office as a Deputy! Beats pulling lumber! 1973, Stephanie Chiharu Nichols was born. Life went on. 1975, Rylen Kazuki Nichols was born. I attend Everett Community College and Central Washington University and graduated with a major in Criminal Justice and a minor in Psychology"

We had our first face-to-face meeting with Philip, Harry, and Heidi and their children in Seattle in June 1995, roughly one year later. In the preceding year we had exchanged a wealth of family photos, phone calls, and letters.

My wife, Gayle, was unable to join me, and I flew out alone, filled with anticipation and apprehension. Harry and his family were driving in from their home in Pittsburg, California. He volunteered to pick me up with his super-sized van, at the Seattle airport. From there we'd proceed to the Seattle Space Needle and our rendezvous with Skippy and his wife Shirin, Heidi, Philip, and their families.

Harry and I recognized each other immediately. He greeted me with a huge bear hug. Delores and their daughters were equally warm and welcoming, but as we climbed into Harry's vintage Chevrolet, I noticed that the family was sending rather skittish looks my way. After exchanging pleasantries about our mutual trips, Harry became strangely quiet. I couldn't imagine what was going on in his mind. A muted sense of shock seemed to fill the air.

Delores would later explain the anxiety I sensed, saying, "We were really spooked, You looked like Nick[4] walking toward us. Nick came back to

---

4   "Nick" was the nickname for Leon, because he was born on Christmas day.

life. We were astounded and shocked. Your gestures and mannerisms were exactly the same. You even talked like him. We were at a loss for words. There could no longer be any doubt that you shared the same father." But Delores's recollection would come much later in the day.

My first real impressions of my new family began to take shape when we reached the Space Needle. We met each other in an excited hubbub of greetings, introductions, and clicking cameras.

My sister, Heidi, was short, plump, and very blonde. My half-brothers were six feet tall, burly and big chested. Harry, outfitted in Levis, a checkered shirt, and boots, looked like a woodsman—except for the pigtail he sported! Philip, a tad taller and quite brawny, stood flanked by Stephanie and Ryland, the beautiful Eurasian children of his former marriage to Chikako. The flesh and blood reality of our mixed and matching extended family seemed quite fanciful—the stuff of imagination. "What," I wondered, "do the children think?" Then it hit me—this was a unique experience for all of us.

It was a clear day, which is unusual for Seattle, and it was certainly an unusual day for us. Our visit to the Space Needle provided incredible views of the snow-capped peaks of Mount Rainier. Everyone was excited; everyone had a camera, and we posed somewhat self-consciously against the stunning backdrop of mountains and bay. For the next hour we played tourists, enjoying the panoramic views of Puget Sound and Port Gardner Bay.

Then we drove to Philip's home in Everett where we tucked into a wonderful meal Delores had prepared: tamales, enchiladas, chili verde, taquitos, rice, and refried beans. We ate and talked and reveled in each other's company. Then we settled in for our first face-to-face family discussion.

There are amazing similarities among us. My brothers look alike, Skippy, Phil, and Harry have the same hair and are fair skinned. I am darker; my hair, like my father's, is straighter and wavy.

We all have the same small ankles and chicken legs. Each of us shares the similarity of a second toe that is longer than the big toe. We all love gardening and history and are addicted to reading science and science fiction.

Harry can go on and on about the movie *Battleship Earth* and how smart L. Ron Hubbard was. Heidi enjoys all the *Star Trek* movies because their topical material explores and extends aspects of race and culture.

Before retiring, Harry was a machinist supervisor in the United States Steel mill in Pittsburg, California. He retired at fifty and now spends his time, gardening, hunting and fishing. He is also trying to patent a state-of-the-art bicycle and runs a local pool for the football and basketball championships. He describes himself quite appropriately as an old hippie, who, as he says, "still hips." Philip, as a Snohomish County deputy sheriff, is a diver who specializes in recovering auto wrecks and narcotic contraband. He is also a specialist in psychological counseling and mediates family disputes.

Philip's girlfriend, Terry Ferguson, an ebullient white woman who worked in the medical examiners office, arrived long after we'd eaten dinner. She'd been involved in extracting someone from a small plane at the crest of a four-thousand-foot mountain. Philip seemed quite happy with her.

It took a while before we got around to discussing the man who had fathered us. Delores, who had been scrutinizing me quite closely, opened that door when she commented on the many similarities between me and Leon. She noted them in my manner of speaking and my gestures; Harry and Philip concurred.

Heidi pondered the wonder and scope of genetic imprinting since I had had so little contact with my father during my lifetime.

When we finally began to talk about Leon Terrenze Nichols,also called "Nick", "Dad", "leon" when we talked about him it was a spirited and emotional discussion. Resentment did not color our conversation. We were all in a state of suspense, full of nervous anticipation and discovery. We realized we'd all been traumatized by Nick, whether by his presence or his absence. We all had stories to tell, feelings to share, old hurts that needed psychic balm, old mysteries that needed to be resolved. We were preparing to piece together the fragments of our lives.

Although Harry still voiced doubts, the black genes seemed more obvious as we looked at each other. We didn't shy away from discussing race. Philip maintained an enigmatic and noncommittal smile. Heidi laughed nervously.

I found it stunning to hear different points of view about one man—a man who had complicated so many lives with his tales and fantasies.

When they were growing up, Leon (called Nick) had shared his love of nature with my half-brothers. He had taken his kids on countless hunting and fishing excursions into the immense backcountry of Utah, Montana, and Washington State. I found myself wishing I had known that life and shared those memories.

Harry recalled how, when he was eight, his father had taught him to drive. "Nick told me if I was old enough to learn to shoot a rifle and hunt, I was old enough to learn to drive."

Dad had an aught-one rifle. Dorothy, their mother, had another. They all hunted together in the wild. Harry would tag along with a .22 and the dog. The dog would drive the deer toward Dad, who would shoot the deer.

These were among the best times Harry had shared with his father. He remembered these experiences fondly and talked of the delight of dining on the venison and fish they caught during these times.

But Leon Terrenze Nichols was many things. He was also a drunk—a mean drunk. Harry, Philip, and Heidi had mentioned Leon's abuse in our phone conversations, but it wasn't until our meeting that they really expressed their deep feelings of anger.

They revisited their memories of Leon as an alcoholic father who frequently abused them and their mother, who as we have read was also an alcoholic and died early.

The more they talked, the more clear it became: the man whom I had longed to nurture and care for me was often a horror to be with. He was both loved and hated by his children. They told many, many stories about Leon that evening.

Heidi said neither Skippy nor I would have gotten to or through medical school, if we'd lived in a household headed by our father.

Heidi shared these remarks eighteen years after our first encounter:

> It's nice to hear from you. Can you believe it will be 18 years since we first met by phone October 31, 1995? Discovery:
> "I was 38 years old then. The phone call from Philip left me astounded. I walked around my house saying "oh my God, oh my God"! I kept thinking how could dad walk away from his wife and two young sons? How could he take that information to his grave?
> It was wonderful to see the photographs you and Skip sent. One of the pictures of you in a white shirt and red sweater was amazing, showing the likeness of dad. If I had seen you walking down the street I might have stood with my mouth hanging open or followed you, thinking you were an apparition of dad."

Leon my father, who also called himself Nick, moved Harry, Philip, and Heidi through twenty-one schools during their childhood. They were constantly relocating—often unexpectedly—Montana to Idaho to Oregon. It seems that Leon would run up debts with his business schemes and then abscond when things got out of hand.

Darryl Lukes and Kenny Garroway, Leon's friends and drinking buddies—whom Harry described as poor rednecks—often traveled with them on these quests for work and new beginnings.

Skippy and I were hearing about another person—someone of whom we had no memory. Reading the letters he had sent to our mother reinforced our childhood memories of him as a warm, loving father, concerned about our family and well-being. As children we'd never known him to be either violent or drunk; he had apparently become a different man over the years. Somehow I had forgotten the night before he left Mother and us on his last visit. I vaguely remember them fighting in their bedroom and my coming in to see mother on the floor crying. I can only imagine that his character had shown up then and would remain with him forever.

Then I remembered the time in the midseventies when Skippy and I had received phone calls from a hysterical Maude.

"Leon called," my mother said, frantically. "He says he wants to spend the winter of his life with me. He even threatened to come back and break the door in if necessary."

Her horror was palpable. She was afraid Leon would return and claim any inheritance she might leave; this meant the Riverside Drive property she owned with her brother, Uncle Eddie. As I counted backward, I concluded that this must have occurred shortly after Dorothy's death. It also meant that she had been in contact with him over the years and would not share the information with us in our search for him.

Mother made me promise not to contact or have anything to do with Leon. I inveigled and persisted until she gave me his telephone number. She relented, but only after I promised not to call him. She made Skippy promise too.

Of course I had to call—and reached a wrong number. But in the meantime, I'd come across *The Wonderful World of Nichols*, a book listing addresses and telephone numbers for everyone named Nichols in the world. It included a Leon Nichols in Washington State.

When a man answered, I put my question to him. "Could you be Leon Nichols, my father?"

"No," he answered immediately and abruptly. "I am German," he said, and then hung up.

Many years later, sitting in my recently discovered half-brother's home, I knew with certainty that my father had been on the other side of that telephone. In fact years later Philip remembered that day! He said Nick was so upset, that they moved out of the house the next day!

When we retired that evening, each of us was filled with a jumble of conflicting emotions. We realized that we dodged a lot of abuse and anger. Mother Maude indeed protected us against what would have indeed affected our lives and our pursuits. She strove to shield us from his malevolence.

We had a mother we loved and respected. She believed in setting and achieving goals. We would never have become doctors without her discipline and support. Our memories of her indomitable spirit and wonderful, strong, and supportive character would always be with us.

The next evening, after a barbequed salmon and saffron rice dinner, we were much more expansive. Heidi arrived with home movies of her 1977 wedding. There she was walking down the aisle on my father's arm. He was seventy-three at the time and looked robust and alert. What a strange sensation to see our father alive and enjoying himself at his daughter's wedding.

The next day, en route to Heidi's home in Mount Vernon, we drove past Broadway Plaza, the last place Leon lived. I got out to take a picture of the sad "bungalow" that they had called home. When we reached Heidi's home, she showed us the obit written by Leon's friends and neighbors.

> Leon Nichols, one of he Broadway Plaza's first and most colorful [sic] residents, was born in Trinidad, Colorado. His father was a seaman and his mother was a senorita born in Barcelona to a family who had received a Spanish land grant in Colorado. Leon attended a technical school in Detroit and worked at night in a garage. About this time, Leon became interested in

radio, and with his genius for anything mechanical, her was soon building crystal and tube radio sets.

At one time, Leon owned and operated a fleet of sixteen taxicabs in New York City, covering the territory between the Battery and Yonkers.

In the early 40's Leon spent a year and a half at the Rock Island Arsenal in Illinois and later served in the South Pacific. Captain Leon Nichols was attached to the First Corps Operation QS and PT offshore rescue boats. He began as an engineer and was soon promoted to chief engineer, serving under General Robert Eichelsberger.

Leon trained several crews of engineers to operate QS patrol boats up and down the Australian coast. He served in almost every theater of operations in the South Pacific and in the Philippines. At Madang, New Guinea, Leon's left arm was shattered by shrapnel and he was hospitalized on a Lurline ship in Oro Bay.

When Leon returned to the States, he lived for a time in San Francisco, married and became a father of three children: Harry who works for U.S. Steel in Pittsburg California, Philip who is a Snohomish County Deputy Sheriff, and Heidi who is employed at Physician's Eye Clinic and Surgical Center in Everett. There are four grandchildren.

This brief account barely scratches the surface of Leon's exciting life. There is no way his accomplishments and adventures can be chronicled in so little space. Everything written here pertaining to Leon's military service is documented and there is much more which should be told. Perhaps one day someone will write a book or make a movie. After all, Leon Nichols is no ordinary man. He is a living legend.

I also realized that with all three, Philip, Heidi, and Harry, there had been a tremendous outpouring of feeling from them. They had been suffering for so long that I was glad they now had an opportunity to talk about their father in a way they had never done before, and to have our sympathy and our empathy as well. Perhaps this whole experience of their discovering their new half-brothers would have a cathartic and therapeutic effect on them.

Visiting Another World ... My Father's Fade to White

I have written about my new family's shock at seeing me and hearing me and talking to me when I arrived in Seattle. I have also written to my half-brother Philip asking him about his growing up with our father. I wondered how my father had made the decision to grow up with them and not with my brother and me in New York. What effect had race played in that decision? The answer went with my father to the grave, but I decided I would ask my siblings about their educations and professional choices and try to puzzle out the question of "nature versus nurture."

What they told us was shocking. They had endured a troubled life with our father. He was a drunk, who never kept a steady job or lived in any place for than two years. The man I had sought to nurture and care for me was a horror to be with. He was both loved and hated by his children. He did give them a love for the outdoors and took them on hunting and fishing trips when they were growing up. I wish I had known that life, and even shared those memories. What irony.

A sunny day in Seattle, which is unique. It was nice to see where Phil and and his girlfriend Terry were living. What is more unique is that it was sunny for the entire time we were in Seattle, a city known for its rainy climate. Well, as they say, "How about that!"

Skippy and I were speechless when we read the obituary. What a great con job Leon had done. Our father just kept reinventing himself and his past, and no one was ever the wiser. He could so easily charm and convince people of anything he wanted them to believe. His stories (of course there was some truth to many of them) and his fantasies were the product of someone who was both indifferent to the effect his behavior had on those around him—those he professed to love—and someone who was his own worst enemy, who had uncontrollable anger and was an alcoholic, who fathered five children (and very likely a few more) and then chose to abandon two of them and mistreat the other three.

The only way I can cope with this sad commentary on who my father was is to keep coming back to the good news—that Skippy and I had the benefit of a wonderful mother and that we both chose our professions and have worked hard doing what we wanted to do. That work has been meaningful and healing, and never once has either one of us regretted our chosen professions.

In retrospect, I'm truly happy that I did keep searching to find Leon because the discovery of Philip, Harry, and Heidi means there is now an extended Nichols family to share our lives with.

Our last day in Washington included a trip to Rosario Beach, which is a beautiful state park on Puget Sound. The waters there abound with large octopuses, bull kelp, and salmon. We ate barbecued oysters—about five dozen! And later in the evening, after consuming an incredible amount of steak, pasta, and salad, we went to the Tulalip Indian Reservation Casino where I indulged in my favorite game, roulette. I had planned to lose no more than $300 but ended up losing $400. Still we had such a good time that I couldn't remember when losing had been so much fun.

Before leaving for home, Philip, Harry, Skippy, and I visited the crematorium at Cypress Lawn Cemetery, where Leon's ashes are interred next to Dorothy's. His site is identified by a simple plaque with an erroneous date of birth.

I thought, "Here lies a man who died in 1989. Skippy and I never saw him for fifty years. He never saw fit to find out how or who we were."

We all held hands, and Philip spoke about the significance of our visit to the cemetery and the terrible emotions it engendered in all of us. I felt the sorrow of finality.

We slept less than two hours that night, having to get up at five o'clock in order to leave at six for the airport. When we all said our good-byes, it was with the promise to keep in close touch, to write, phone, and visit each other, especially at holiday time and during summer vacations.

Once we were home, Skippy and I didn't discuss the Seattle visit until a few weeks later. We both had a great deal to think about and needed to sift through our feelings. The visit did serve as a fitting closure to our father's absence and rediscovery. But I was left with so many mixed emotions too. I couldn't fathom why he had chosen to live with that part of the family and not with us. Was it a racial preference? Was it only because he and my mother didn't get along? Then again, as much as I would have liked to know what was going on in his mind—and heart—when it came to reasons for the abandonment, I can only feel tremendous relief that I matured, developed, and prospered in spite of his absence, and that me and my brother were spared the lies, the abuse, and the tragedy of having an alcoholic father (and mother!). Those scars can take a lifetime to heal. I suppose you have to play the hand you're dealt.

Chapter Thirteen

REFLECTIONS

And so, as Skippy and I have discovered, we now have not only more family, but a more racially mixed family. I've always been a proponent of multiracialism and multiculturalism. My immediate family is content to call themselves multiracial, reflecting the various European, African, and American Indian blood that courses through our veins. In fact, we generally check off all three racial classifications that appear on various applications whenever we have to fill them out! And I suggest that others do this too so that we and those others can truly celebrate our racial and cultural diversity. It is, after all, the reason this country was created, and it is still what makes us great, and our people strong.

The Other Kids Had Fathers

Unfortunately there are not many fragments of memory regarding my father, but there have been fantasies of a make-believe father. I might have imagined that my mother's boyfriends were surrogates. I remember Capt. Ted Thompson and Sy MacArthur. My brother later complained that Mother always picked "losers." Ted was married and had a son, and Si was a "confirmed bachelor," and chief steward on the SS *United States*.

The fathers of the other kids I knew were no role models. Most were drunks, weak minded, wimps—or even all three. Most had little influence over their children's life or development. Others were struggling with their own demons, angry at not having reached any level of their ability. Later I did have some psychological and professional support from Dr. John Moseley, the father of one of my early girlfriends, who took an interest in my development, as well that of another friend, John Norton. In fact we both became doctors and are very close friends even now. We had little contact with the fathers on the block. Most lived lives isolated from the others. There were never any block or neighborhood parties.

What I Didn't Learn from a Father

Who was my father as a man? Well, from the letters that he wrote to his wife, I think he sincerely loved her and indeed he loved his children. What I wanted most was clarity. I wanted to know why he left us when we were so young, especially when he professed his love for his two sons in his letters to our mother. I wanted to know or understand why he never tried to write us or contact us when we were growing up. I wanted to know or understand why he denied our existence even after I telephoned and talked to him in Washington State.

I wanted him to know how much we needed what I felt was his strength, his courage, and his ambition. I looked for guidance and direction and found none from him. I never got to read his letters to my mother, so I couldn't even hang on to those thoughts. I wonder what went through my mother's mind that caused her to withhold information. After graduating from medical school, I thought I had done all that by myself without any support from him. I had a school loan from the state of New York and got some money from my mother as she could or would send it. Oh yes, I was bitter about not having a father to shield, protect, and strengthen me. I covered my ego with conceit and arrogance— proud of what I had accomplished in spite of all and ahead of all. No one on the planet had done what I had done before me. But my idle boasts were to be shattered by wisdom. It became quite apparent that other black men have risen to the occasion under similar, if not worse, circumstances and that I owe a lot of people for making it possible. It took me a while to learn this.

I wanted to hear from my father why he chose to raise those children as white in Washington State and thereabouts instead of his brown children in the Bronx. Why did he choose to raise them instead of Skippy and me? I wondered about that as I met them and talked to them. Why did he chose them over us? How ironic to find that he treated them so badly. He imparted no traditions, no oral history, to my brother and me. We had no positive family history from my father to pass down to our grandchildren. We had no reputation to uphold. We had no family standard to measure ourselves with. (But, on the other hand, having been free of this, we had no bounds and could soar as high as the eagles, my favorite bird.)

I wonder now that I didn't cry more often about not having a father around when all the other children did—or not getting presents from him on Christmas or birthdays. I took the lie that was told to us as the truth—that he was away in the army. Early on, no reason was given for his not being home. Still, later, he had just left one day never to return. We never asked why he didn't come back or try to contact us. We accepted life as it came.

From what we later learned from his other family (my half-brothers and half-sister), it seems it would have been a disaster to have had him living with us as our dad. He was a drunk and an abuser of his wife and his children, who suffered large mental wounds from their living with him. It is so ironic that we did so much "better" professionally than our Western counterparts. We suffered less from his presence. We would have loved to have shared the more pleasant things they shared with our father, for example, his taking them on trips in the wilderness to hunt, camp, and fish all over the Northwest and Montana.

Was It Really "Like Father, Like Son"?

I missed the wealth of information that my father could have given me. I could have learned from his stories of growing up. I could have shared his wisdom about diesel engines and motors. I could have grown up to be an engineer or even own a garage.

The search for Leon Terrenze Nichols was a profoundly painful and powerful life lesson. We had heard many stories of the personal see-saws of our father's life and times. We have certainly been bedeviled by the actions of his life. But the truth remains that I still have very little knowledge of just who Leon Terrenze Nichols was.

I continue to have many questions about the why of my father, his background and motivations, his happiness, failures and provocations. What formed him? How did he think? From what source did his personal demons, fears, and insecurities spring?

Filling in the emotional blanks and uncovering the hidden chambers of Leon's life would undoubtedly take many years. Today our primary charge is to continue to become more firmly family—to close the gaps between our conflicting memories of this man and to be the healthiest family we can be. In that process we honor what was worthy and honorable in his blood and in his spirit. This is my story of becoming that family.

Chapter Fourteen

LIVING WITH THE SHOCK

What must my new family be thinking? Are we black?

I often wonder what they must have thought to find out that we were black and also considered their father black. They had grown up thinking he was white. Now I wonder if they think he was black, and if so, whether they now think they are black too.

This news must have been a jolt to them. I wonder how they feel now after the five years of this revelation. I wonder if they had ever discussed this with their in-laws and friends. I wonder how it has shaped their lives. I will have to frame a thought or letter to them so see if they have any insights on this question.

Here are some isolated thoughts that I have regarding our Western counterparts concerning what they considered their ethnic identity. Some of these impressions may be contradictory, but bear with me. I don't think they thought of themselves as pure Caucasians or Aryan. Not even a glance at their father would indicate to them that he was a mongrel a muttof some type. However, I don't think they considered him black in the sense of him having African genes. Without a doubt they swallowed his yarn about his Spanish genes (land grant and all that), but I don't understand how they could imagine our supposed grandfather, standing by the schoolyard fence in that photo, as Germanic. And on top of that, the fence was allegedly near a concentration camp, which they ought to have noticed didn't contain anyone—and this was supposed to have been rather late in the war when it should have been crammed with all sorts of sufferers.

Perhaps this image of the grandfather conveniently matched their mother's ancestry and assured a mostly Germanic background to offset the rather pesky heritage of some Spanish past. With this in mind, there is no reason from them to consider themselves black. On reflection, people with Spanish or Latin ancestry are not considered black. The two boys could look at themselves and surmise that they might be some white mixture but certainly not black. When Heidi was born, there was further incontrovertible proof that indeed they were a white family. They wanted to overlook the fact that their hair texture was a bit suspicious and that the only way that could have occurred was that at some point in their genomic past, even long past, someone had a "touch of the tar." They probably didn't dwell on that, thinking that curliness can occur spontaneously in Caucasians. I'm not aware of any Caucasian group with so-called kinky hair that has not had some historic contact with Africans at sometime in the past, no matter how remote. At any rate, I don't see why they should have considered themselves black. Even the military didn't think Dad was black, but I'm sure something else akin to white and comfortably passable. So all of the whiteness stacks up in their favor.

Nevertheless, the whites in their neighborhood were not so bamboozled. Since they—Dad and the two boys—were quite a bit different looking than those in Minnesota and Montana where they lived, trouble often erupted. They were called "nigger," and to believe them, their house was burned down. Well that's the American way, and I'm sure that must have shocked the crap out of them and caused them to reflect on those days and call anyone who had a different hue than them a nigger. As such, the worrisome seed had to be planted in their beings. I don't think it festered; but there it was, and they probably didn't discuss it together very often.

What does one do when one feels white? You hate blacks, and this is what Harry did. I know this because one of the daughters told me so. I can't speak for Philip, although I'm sure he felt a tinge of doubt given the fact that his girlfriend, Terry, told me she spent a considerable amount of time trying to convince their fellow workers that Philip was not black. (All her efforts were shattered when we appeared.) I'm sure Heidi had no doubt as to who she was. There were probably many other episodes, in at least the boys' lives, where racism was an issue. Much to their disbelief, given their understanding of their background, they probably thought it was a mistaken belief, and they shook it off. What do I believe they feel now? Well, no matter what they felt, they have seen us, and the identity of our genes cannot be denied. Having a common father certainly does help them face the truth to a wee bit of African genes in the pool. I feel, however, that most of our (Skippy's and my) African genes came from Mother. But Dad certainly had them also. I feel that, reluctantly, they had to accept the truth and don't think of it anymore. Jessica Steve's daughter has married a nice young, black guy, Mike Kidd, and now it's all in the family.

Parenthetically, I feel that simply having an infinitesimal amount of "black genes" in one's gene pool does not qualify one to be called black. Most of the people we know are such a mixture of all different races it is a shame that they cannot be classified simply a mélange as an official racial type. I think it is beautiful to think of oneself that way. This mélange lives all over the world and is sometime called Egyptian, Lebanese, Tunisian, or other names, depending on the particular passport. They certainly have African genes somewhere, but they do not qualify to be called black or white. They are part everyone and have their own identity.

Chapter Fifteen

GETTING TO KNOW THEM

I will write about the relationships with the new-found family and their thoughts about finding a new family on the East Coast. We differ so much because of our separate development, but we share many traits and feelings.

We are actively in contact by telephone and have visited each other on different occasions. We participated in the marriage of Steve and Delores's daughter. Our telephone calls usually occur around the holidays and birthdays. We have long conversations, keeping up with each other's children and our health. We discussed plans for future vacations together. In fact we are all going to be together in Puerto Vallarta In November 2000. Because of research for the book, I have written questions by email about their impressions of our first meeting in 1995.

I have recently tried to get into discussions of current politics, but these issues are skirted by Philip. He doesn't want me to mail him any forwarded jokes on e-mail. He says he wants to use the e-mail to get to know us better, but he since then hasn't written any thoughts except for what he has written below. I am sure he will in the future. It is not easy to close the gap of fifty years. We have no memories to fall back on. "Remember when" doesn't come up.

A door has closed, and another door has opened. We are all living with the information now. I consider the ironies concerning whether it would have been wise to know my father while we were growing up. My father remained out of our life for fifty years. On balance it seems that the negative effect he had on his second set of children was balanced by the positive effect that Mother Maude had on my brother and me.

He was, however, not quite hermetic. I did manage to get a call to him in Everett, and he had his chance to deny us again. My mother was also insistent on keeping us from knowing him; and she was adamant about this to the end.

I have noticed in the practice that my casual questions about parentage and upbringing reveal that many people in America have grown up without a father's presence. There are many reasons for these breakups: divorce, separation, death. But the fact remains there is a distinct problem to be dealt with.

Philip sent this note by e-mail on March 5, 2006:

> "70 is not old, it is a perspective. A place where time and experience merge to clear ones sight. A reflection pool where all of our experiences balance and we reach a place where everything matters and nothing matters. We understand the why. When I look back on everything that has happened, I don't always like what occurred but see how it formed and developed me as a whole person. Life being eternal makes me realize this is just one segment of many. How else would we know what it is to be human than to experience it first hand. I remember when I used to hate both Dad and Mom. Now I see where if one thing they did was different—I would be different. Thing is I like who I am and thank them for their influence. You are very much like Dad. Of all of us you mirror him the most. If you ever are curious what he was like in the absent time look in the mirror. You lived a different reality as did the rest of us. I on occasion wondered what it would be like to be a Dr.? I see the healer in myself and realize my training

took a different course but arrived at the same outcome. In the time you have left your priorities are clear. You can not take the material only the memories. What you leave behind in material is not as important as the memories you leave for others. Any where in your heart where there is an awareness of a need to make amends, now is the only time you have to do so. Meeting you and Skip filled an enormous information gap. I understand Dad a lot better than before. Last night I had a dream with him in it. Not sure yet what all the symbolism was but for sure he is ok and sending messages. You know none of us are getting out of here alive:) My sense is that he will be waiting on the other side and we will get the rest of the story as they say. I wish you and I could spend more time together physically because it is more personal than e-mail. But this is cool. Keep writing. Phil J"

This meant a lot to me, for various reasons, none more important than that he felt that meeting us meant so much to him in trying to understand their father and their own lives. I certainly will get back to him about our feelings about knowing them and wondering how they could have been so much more like us. We should have known our younger brothers, to show them what we thought and hoped to be. They are certainly mentally equipped to be the doctors that Philip had wondered about. Life has many roads and mazes. There is so little time to be here with them. We must make many more efforts to share our thoughts. For in that deep of oblivion to which we all shall go, what ideas can be shared? And to what purpose?

Heidi sent this note recently:

"When you and Skip came to meet us in Washington, it was wonderful to have a large part of dad's past history filled in. I remember Phil, Harry, and I sitting across the table from you and being stunned at your mannerisms that were exactly like dad's. The way you sat, crossed your legs, used your hands while you spoke, and even enunciated your words. You are simply a younger version of him.

The following summer Skip and [his wife] Shirin brought me to New York. I never dreamed I would go there. It wasn't what I had expected and I found it to be quite beautiful. Skip, Shirin and you generously showed me around the city. We had barbeques at both your homes. You generously arranged for a limousine ride for Meredith and me and took us to Tavern On the Green for dinner and we ate dessert at The Birdland Jazz Club. We also took a carriage ride through Central Park and Crown Heights Promenade.

But the most important part of the trip was meeting my nieces and nephew, sitting and talking with you and Skip, and hearing both your experiences with dad. Looking at pictures and going to the neighborhood and house you all lived in and the places he worked. It helped fill in a lot of blanks in his stories and even explain some pictures we had possession of. Dad was an enigma to me. I knew very little about his past and he didn't like to talk about it. Even when I tried to get information such as a birth certificate from Colorado, where he said he was born, they had no documentation. It was as if he had crawled from under a rock at low tide. All we had were the stories he told us.

When you told us your experiences of life with dad, they were so different and even opposite of what I experienced. Dad's alcoholism made him very violent. I now believe he drank to dull the shame of abandoning his family in N.Y. I can understand that you are angry and may never forgive him for abandoning you and Skip. While I, throughout my childhood, wished and prayed he would just go away and never return.

However, as an adult and through receiving professional counseling, my own personal experiences and journey in life, and developing my own spiritual foundation, I have forgiven him for all of the emotional, psychological and physical abuse he inflicted on me and my mother. Fortunately, I was never sexually abused.

In many ways, growing up with two alcoholic parents, one of them very violent, has made me a strong and independent woman. Yet, I am still working through my own issues of fear and mistrust of men.

Ultimately, I choose not to live in the past. I believe we are all spiritual beings having human experiences. We are here to teach, to learn, and to grow through our experiences with one another. Forgiveness and unconditional love to our self and each other are the most important lessons to learn."

EPILOGUE

Writing this memoir, which I have worked on since 1994, has been very cathartic for me. As with all lives, there have been times of happiness and joy and other times of sadness and depression.

This project has given me many hours of quiet reflection and in the end prepared me in a strange way for the end of my days. These are but brief glimpses of my life and the lives of others who are near and dear to me.

I have done well in my profession and raising my daughters. I trust they will tell their grandchildren something about me. Life goes on.

Sure, when I was decades younger I tried to play golf and tennis, went skiing, went scuba diving in the Caribbean, zip lining in Hawaii, and mountain climbing in Colorado. I tried most everything and learned quickly that it takes twenty years of practice to be an expert. I never got past novice in any of those past pursuits. Now I play Words with Friends and video games like *Age of Empires*. I watch sports like football and baseball in season; HBO series like *Boardwalk Empire* and *Game of Thrones*; *Let's Make a Deal*; and of course CNN.

We played Trivial Pursuit, poker, Monopoly, and Scrabble with the kids as they grew up in the house. And later when they left, I would spend the time at home in the den and sunroom looking at the bookcases filled with so many fictional, reference, and historical books and binders that held my life's information and secrets. I transferred many of the photos in the albums to the computer. All of the music was put in storage of the computer cloud. I am sure I am not alone in this regard.

We continue to be a family in spite of Leon's keeping us apart for so long. All of us feel so much better knowing each other. We are a family.

Philip wrote on March 5, 2006:

I think a lot of what he wrote then is worth repeating. It helps me to understand so much about my life and also his. I have excerpted a few sentences that have much meaning. I was shocked to read. *You are very much like Dad. Of all of us you mirror him the most. If you ever are curious what he was like in the absent time look in the mirror.* Because I cannot fathom how that could be, or how Phil can think that way. I certainly don't think I would be as violent and mean as he seemed to have been. I wonder what else he saw in Nick that he has not shared with us. I do understand how Phil could have become a doctor. I am impressed to read. *I on occasion wondered what it would be like to be a Dr.? I see the healer in myself and realize my training took a different course but arrived at the same outcome*

. Meeting you and Skip filled an enormous information gap. I understand Dad a lot better than before. Last night I had a dream with him in it. Not sure yet what all the symbolism was but for sure he is ok and sending messages.

This meant a lot to me, for various reasons, none more important than his feelings that meeting us meant so much to him in trying to understand their father and then their lives. I certainly will get back to him on our feelings about knowing them and wondering how they could have been so more like us. We should have known our younger brothers to show them what we thought and hoped to be. They are certainly mentally equipped to be the Doctors that Philip had wondered about. Life has many roads and mazes. There is so little time to be here with them. We must make many more efforts to share our thoughts. For in that deep of oblivion to which we all shall go, what ideas can be shared? And to what purpose?

Recently, Harry (whose first name is actually Steve)said he would send me his thoughts about our getting together.

"A lot of this is new to me. I never knew that he had had confrontations about race when he was a little boy, although Philip alluded to some events in his growing up. I was amazed to hear of his thoughts of race when he was an apprentice. We are still getting to know each other. I look forward to more letters."

He wrote this last year and I do want to add this letter from Steve. It is so poignant and expressive.

Eddie 12-13-13

I don't know where to begin this letter so I will just start typing and let it develop.

It will probably take a day or 2 or more to get what I want to say and how to respond to your thoughts, observations, and impressions of me and the west coast Nichols.

Again forgive me for this delayed response. My life or should I say my partners life has been turned upside down for the past year and a half. She has been diagnosed as bi-polar and her mind has short-circuited and the vibrant, talented, well rounded woman who I fell in love with has disappeared into a fearful, mentally ill person whom has lost her faith. Consciousness and memories of all that she learned in life. I am in service to her 24/7 dealing with her doctors, business, family & friends and trying to rehabilitate her.

First of all I want to say I enjoyed meeting You and Skip and the time we shared together most of all being with You, Skip, & Phil and doing our war / peace dance on dads grave forgiving him for taking his silence to the other side and leaving us to wonder why and how a man this man could be so wounded and show so little love and affection to his own blood.

In some ways I think you and skip are the luckier of his children. I always wanted a normal life whatever that is/was instead of the violent abusive environment I grew up in. Did you ever experience his violence other than the abandonment he instilled in your psyche? Someday I would like to sit down and talk to the 2 of you about our life stories. I wonder and would like to know the truth about the 2 girls that you were introduced as sisters to you when you were a child. I would also like to find out about our Grandparents on dads side (some of the papers skip sent [war records] me have addresses of where they lived prior to coming to New York.

A little of my own personal history. I experienced my first racial slur when I was called a mulatto when I was 9 years, didn't even know what the word meant except for the tonality used by this person who I thought was a friend hurt and confused, and made me angry at the time.

I never really experienced that again (lived and grew up as a poor little white boy in a totally dysfunctional home) until I was in early 20s when I let my hair grow long and became the resident outcast hippy during my machinist apprenticeship at US Steel. They wanted to fire me for my political / social views (I was involved in the civil rights movement and the anti-war protests) but couldn't because I carried straight A-s in my class and shop work and my best friend was their token black affirmative action apprentice at the time. I knew early on that on my mom's side that I was part Indian and never was prejudiced toward anyone. I was always outspoken and supportive of people who were used or taken advantage of, and the Black and Mexican men and women I worked with encouraged me to run and supported me for the 25 years I served as a union officer.

Again I apologize for taking so long to respond to your letters. Hopefully later on, after Elaine heals I will have more time to communicate with you.

So this is the ongoing story. I hope it will continue and grow. One day, I will write an update on what has happened in the past twenty years, but that is another story.

ACKNOWLEDGMENTS

I would like to acknowledge those who have been so helpful to me in writing my memoir. First my brothers and my sister in New York, Washington, and California, especially Leon T. Nichols, MD, who has expressed his thoughts about growing up and with whom I have developed a true and lasting friendship in our old age. I felt obliged to include his thoughts, which at times differ from mine. Steve (Harry) Nichols of Pittsburg, California, who has told many stories about his growing up with Dad. Philip Nichols from Osa, Washington, who has written long letters about his growing up with our father. He has supported my efforts and thoughts to join our families and live together. Heidi Nichols, our beloved sister, who has endured life and is evolving every day. We, her brothers, love her.

Thanks also to:

My daughters, including Christiana Celeste Nichols, MD, my middle daughter, who has inspired me to write and live in my old age, and Meredith McKenzie Nichols, my youngest daughter, who is my clone in attitude and character. I love her energy, her joie de vivre.

Of course June Leslie Holcomb-Nichols, my lovely young bride, who has put up with my burdens and supported me in my efforts to stay young, spirited, and alive. We were married at home by Rev. Calvin Butts II in February 2012. We are still on our honeymoon.

There are other friends, old and new, who have been valuable in focusing my thoughts about the characters that have influenced me.

Maurus Vogel, my eternal friend, who now lives in Lugano, Switzerland, has helped with memories of our university days and medical education, and who urged me to reflect on all that happened to us in Switzerland, and with whom I shared a lot of time together in the south of France, where we still meet to enjoy life.

Irene Schindler, my neighbor and friend, who helped me organize my thoughts and dig into my feelings. Her writing experience has taught me so much in the last ten years.

The ladies whom I have known since my adolescent years—Toni Des Verney Bennett, Jane Moseley, and Toni Willis Brown—whose great memories helped with recreating my thoughts of the teenage years.

Shirley Hilliman, who became a school principal in Massachusetts, made me aware of the lives of our "village" of Fish Avenue. Her details of the families were so incisive.

Sergio A. Lopez, my technical support, without whom this book would not be possible. My friend and neighbor helped me throughout the process of publishing this memoir.

Documents: War record information came from the Department of Defense, the P.T. records i.e. P.T.. Boats Inc, Insurance documents. Including New York Life Insurance and the Social Security Department. Historical facts about Basel and its history and Columbia University came from *Wikipedia*.

Above all, my diaries, which I have kept forever, revealed my thoughts, hopes, and feelings and kept me aware of memories and events in my life that had meaning.